# PESTICIDES

CODE OF PRACTICE FOR USING PLANT
PROTECTION PRODUCTS IN SCOTLAND

code of practice has been prepared jointly by the Scottish
ecutive Environment and Rural Affairs Department and the
Health and Safety Commission (HSC).

ISBN: 0-7559-5093-3

Scottish Executive
St Andrew's House
Edinburgh
EH1 3DG

Produced for the Scottish Executive by Astron B46884 12-06

Published by the Scottish Executive, December, 2006

Further copies are available from

Blackwell's Bookshop
53 South Bridge
Edinburgh
EH1 1YS

The text pages of this document are printed on recycled paper and are 100% recyclable

# CONTENTS

# CONTENTS

# CONTENTS

Page

# CONTENTS

# CONTENTS

Page

# CONTENTS

# TABLES

# EMERGENCY PROCEDURES

## YOUR EMERGENCY ACTION PLAN SHOULD CONSIDER HOW TO PROTECT THE ENVIRONMENT WHEN YOU ARE DEALING WITH ANY EXPOSURE OR SPILLAGE.

### A1 ACTION PLANS

Anyone who uses pesticides professionally (that is, as part of their job) must be trained in emergency procedures and must have, and understand, their own action plans. These emergency action plans should be kept up to date to cover new equipment or new ways of working. Many product labels will have specific advice on what to do if you are contaminated or there is a spillage or fire. This information is always on the manufacturer's material safety data sheet (MSDS), which you can get when you buy the product.

### A2 PERSONAL CONTAMINATION

You can be exposed to pesticides through your skin (usually the main route of exposure) and eyes, by breathing them in or by swallowing them. Your emergency action plan should consider how to protect the environment when you are dealing with any exposure or spillage.

If you, or people you are working with or nearby, feel unwell when you are using pesticides, or after you have used them, you should do the following:

↘ Stop work and, if necessary, call for medical help immediately.

↘ Prevent further exposure. Use appropriate personal protective equipment when helping a contaminated person or handling contaminated surfaces.

↘ Move the casualty away from the source of contamination and remove all their contaminated clothing.

↘ Wash contaminated skin or hair thoroughly with plenty of clean water.

↘ If eyes are contaminated, immediately flush them with plenty of clean running water. Then cover the eye with a sterile eye pad or similar lint-free dressing.

↘ If someone has swallowed a pesticide, do not try to make them vomit (be sick) unless the product label recommends this.

↘ Make the casualty rest and keep them warm.

↘ If the casualty is unconscious, check their breathing and pulse and put them in the recovery position. If there are no signs of breathing or a pulse, begin CPR (cardiopulmonary resuscitation), if necessary, using a method of artificial respiration which will avoid the risk of you swallowing or breathing in the pesticide.

↘ Give the doctor or hospital a copy of the product labels and material safety data sheets. If this is not possible, give them details of the active ingredients and the product names.

↘ Make sure you or someone else reports the incident to your nearest Health and Safety Executive (HSE) office. The address and phone number will be in *The Phone Book* or you can phone the HSE 'Info line' on 0845 3450055. For out-of-hours emergencies, phone the HSE on 0151 9229235.

## A3 DEALING WITH SPILLAGE

You can keep the negative effect a pesticide spillage has on the environment as low as possible by carrying an appropriate 'spill kit' and knowing how to use it. You must never hose down spilt pesticide or allow it to enter surface water, ditches, drains or soakaways. It is good practice to have a diagram of your drainage systems available for emergencies.

If you spill any pesticide as a concentrate, ready-to-use product or spray solution, no matter how small the spill is, you should do the following:

↘ Keep people and animals away from the affected area until the situation has been dealt with.

↘ Avoid becoming contaminated yourself. Wear appropriate personal protective equipment.

↘ Immediately prevent further spillage using, for example, an emergency folding pool.

↘ Contain the spilt material. As a priority, keep the contamination away from surface water, ditches and drains.

↘ Tell the Scottish Environment Protection Agency (phone 0800 807060) and warn others at risk if the spill:

- contaminates any water;

- could contaminate water later, either directly or through a drainage system; or

- contaminates a large amount of soil.

↘ You may need to tell neighbours or people using the water downstream of the spill.

↘ Tell Scottish Water (phone 0845 6008855) if the spill enters a sewage system.

↘ For spilt liquids, put absorbent material, such as cat litter or dry sand, around the spill and use the same material to soak up the spillage. The material you use must be 'inert'. This means it must not cause any chemical reaction.

↘ Sweep up any solids and material used to contain liquid spills. Sweep up as gently as possible without raising dust. Then sprinkle the area with inert absorbent material and sweep gently again.

↘ For leaking containers, do one of the following:

- Use the contents immediately.

- Pour the contents of the damaged container into an empty container that originally held the same product. The container should be in good condition and with an undamaged label.

- Put the leaking container into a suitable larger container clearly labelled with the product name and the hazard classification and risk and safety phrases shown on the product label.

↘ Never put any pesticides into an empty food or drink container.

↘ Dispose of all contaminated material safely and legally (for example, through a licensed waste-disposal contractor). This includes getting rid of any equipment which you used to clean up the spillage and which cannot be decontaminated safely.

## A4 SUSPECTED ANIMAL POISONING

If you find a creature or animal which you suspect has been affected by being exposed to pesticides, or if you find spilt pesticide or unprotected baits, you should do the following (as appropriate):

↘ Get the animal away from the source of contamination, taking care not to be contaminated yourself. If necessary, wear appropriate personal protective equipment.

↘ Take the animal to a vet or contact a vet immediately, keeping the animal sheltered and resting.

↘ If possible, give the vet the product labels. Otherwise, give the name of the products and their active ingredients.

↘ Phone the Wildlife Incident Investigation Scheme (WIIS) on 0800 321 600 for an incident involving any creature (except fish). This means not only wild mammals, birds and pets but also bees or other insects, worms and other creatures.

↘ For incidents involving fish, phone the Scottish Environment Protection Agency on 0800 807060.

↘ Do not touch any dead animals, unprotected baits, pesticides or containers, and never try to unblock a badger sett or fox earth which may have been gassed.

↘ If it is safe to do so, cover any dead animals or pesticides until they can be disposed of or safely removed to be analysed.

## A5 FIRE

If you discover a fire that involves pesticides, you should do the following:

↘ **For small fires** which you can deal with quickly, safely and without causing a significant risk of exposure to fumes or other material produced by burning pesticides, use appropriate firefighting equipment.

↘ **In all other circumstances**, call the fire brigade and the police, and follow your evacuation procedures. Warn other people who may be at risk (for example, if fumes are blowing in their direction).

↘ Give the fire brigade a complete and accurate list of the products involved and their active ingredients.

↘ Deal with any spilt pesticides resulting from the fire or firefighting activities as described above.

# FOREWORD

# A MESSAGE FROM ROSS FINNIE, MINISTER FOR ENVIRONMENT AND RURAL DEVELOPMENT

'I am happy to give my full support to the new Code of Practice for using Plant Protection Products in Scotland. The new Code replaces the "Green Code" (Code of Practice for the Safe Use of Pesticides on Farms and Holdings) which has been an important source of practical advice for farmers, crofters and growers on how to use pesticides safely and, by doing so, to meet the legal obligations which cover the use of pesticides.

The new Code reflects Scottish Executive policy to reduce to the lowest possible level the effect of pesticide use on people, wildlife, plants and the environment while making sure that pests, diseases and weeds are effectively controlled. Many of the environmental protection schemes launched under the Voluntary Initiative represent current best practice and the benefits of these and other measures are explained in the Code.

As well as bringing the advice in the old "Green Code" up to date, the Scottish Executive have taken this opportunity to widen the scope of the Code to cover all plant protection uses of pesticides. By doing this, we have aimed to produce a single publication which will be relevant and of practical value to all professional users of pesticides in agriculture, horticulture, amenity situations and forestry.

I thank everyone who has contributed ideas and comments both before and during the public consultation period. I believe, we have produced an up to date and readable document which will encourage best practice whenever plant protection products are used.'

SCOTTISH EXECUTIVE

Scottish Executive Environment and Rural Affairs Department
Pentland House
47 Robb's Loan
Edinburgh
EH14 1TY

# NOTICES

6 : PESTICIDES

## C1 GENERAL NOTICE UNDER FOOD AND ENVIRONMENT PROTECTION ACT 1985 AND THE HEALTH AND SAFETY AT WORK ETC ACT 1974

This code comes into effect on 3 July 2006. On that date it will replace all previous editions of the Code of Practice for the Safe Use of Pesticides on Farms and Holdings.

It will also replace:

⬐ parts of the approved code of practice for the safe use of pesticides for non-agricultural purposes that relate to using pesticides in amenity and forestry situations; and

⬐ the voluntary code of practice for the use of pesticides in amenity and industrial areas.

## C2 NOTICE OF ISSUING THIS CODE UNDER SECTION 17 OF THE FOOD AND ENVIRONMENT PROTECTION ACT 1985

This code of practice has been prepared for professionals who use plant protection products. It gives practical guidance on part III of the Food and Environment Protection Act 1985 (FEPA) and, in particular, the regulations under that part of the act controlling how plant protection products are used in Scotland.

As required by section 17 of FEPA, Ministers have consulted organisations which represent the interests of everyone concerned.

## C3 NOTICE OF THIS CODE BEING APPROVED BY THE HEALTH AND SAFETY COMMISSION UNDER SECTION 16 OF THE HEALTH AND SAFETY AT WORK ETC ACT 1974

Under Section 16(1) of the Health and Safety at Work etc. Act 1974 (HSWA), and with the Secretary of State's consent, the Health and Safety Commission has approved the paragraphs of this code as listed below which relate to the health and safety of people at work, or people who may be affected by the activities of people at work.

The following paragraphs of this code are approved to provide practical guidance on controlling exposure to pesticides at work under the Control of Substances Hazardous to Health Regulations 2002 (COSHH) (SI 2002 Number 2677).

| | |
|---|---|
| Annex C, glossary 1 | the meaning of 'approval', 'consent' and 'user' |
| Paragraph 1.4 | The official status of the code |
| Paragraphs 3.4.1, 3.4.2, 3.4.3 (except 3rd clause and its bullet points), 3.4.4, 3.4.5, 3.4.6 and 3.4.7 | Regulation 6: assessment |
| Paragraphs 3.5.1, 3.5.2 (except 3rd clause), 3.5.5 (except from 5th clause to end), 3.5.6 (1st clause) 3.5.6 (3rd clause onwards), 3.5.8 and 3.7.4 | Regulation 7: controlling exposure |
| Paragraphs 3.5.6 (last clause) and 3.5.7 (1st clause) | Regulation 8: using control measures |
| Paragraphs 3.5.7 (2nd clause to 5th clause) | Regulation 9: maintenance responsibilities |
| Paragraphs 3.6.1 and 6.6 | Regulation 10: monitoring exposure |
| Paragraphs 3.6.2 (except 2nd clause and its bullet points), 3.6.3 (except the third and last clauses), 3.6.4, 3.6.5 (except last clause) and 6.8 (1st clause and its bullet points) | Regulation 11: health surveillance |
| Paragraphs 2.1, 2.2 and 2.3 | Regulation 12: information, instructions and training |

The definitions in this code are also approved where they are defining words or phrases used in the paragraphs above.

Signed:

Secretary to the Health and Safety Commission

Date: 25 May 2006

# INTRODUCTION

# A PEST, WEED OR DISEASE BEING PRESENT DOES NOT JUSTIFY TAKING ACTION AGAINST IT.

## 1.1 HOW DO I DECIDE IF IT IS NECESSARY TO USE A PESTICIDE?

Using pesticides incorrectly can put people and the environment at risk. If you use a pesticide when you don't need to you will be wasting money and increasing the possibility of pests becoming resistant. In some cases you might also damage the treated area. A pest, weed or disease being present does not justify taking action against it.

For these reasons, you should take care when deciding whether or not to use a pesticide.

↘ Identify the special weed, disease or pest affecting the area you are concerned about.

↘ Ask yourself whether you need to use a pesticide or whether there is another method of control or combination of methods you could use.

↘ Consider the financial loss, damage or visual effect caused by the pest, weed or disease and whether this outweighs the cost of using the pesticide.

↘ Consider whether the doses or concentrations of pesticides being used might damage the area being treated or the next crop planted there.

↘ Ask yourself whether you can make these decisions yourself or whether you need someone to help.

↘ If you decide to use a pesticide, plan how to use it properly. Is it possible to reduce the amount you use or the area you apply it to?

## 1.2 WHAT ADVICE IS GIVEN IN THIS CODE?

This code of practice explains how you can use pesticides and plant protection products safely and so meet the legal conditions which cover their use.

The term 'plant protection product' is defined in the Plant Protection Products (Scotland) Regulations 2005, regulation 2. It means a substance or preparation that contains one or more 'active' ingredients (in the form in which it is supplied to the user) which are intended to:

↘ Protect plants or plant products against all harmful organisms or prevent the action of those organisms;

↘ Influence the processes of plants, other than as a nutrient (for example, to regulate growth);

↘ Preserve plant products (except for substances or products which are controlled under European Union law on preservatives);

↘ Destroy unwanted plants; or

↘ Destroy parts of plants or control or prevent the undesired growth of plants.

The term 'pesticides' is defined in the Control of Pesticides Regulations 1986 (as amended by the Control of Pesticide (Amendment) Regulations 1997), regulation 3. Briefly, it means any substance, preparation or organism that is prepared for or used to control any pest. A pest is any unwanted plant, harmful creature, or organism that is harmful to plants, wood or other plant products.

Throughout this code we use the term 'pesticide' to cover pesticides and plant protection products. 'Pesticides' and 'plant protection products' are herbicides (products to kill weeds and other unwanted plants), insecticides (products to kill bugs), molluscicides (products to kill slugs and snails), vertebrate control agents (products that control small animals and birds, such as rodenticides, which kill rats and mice) and so on. **Table 1** overleaf lists everything covered by this code.

# 1.3 WHAT DOES THIS CODE COVER?

**TABLE 1** This code covers everything listed below

| Edible crops (including treating the seed, the growing crop and the harvested crop) | Non-edible crops | Non-crop uses |
|---|---|---|
| ↘ **All edible agricultural and horticultural crops** (outdoor and protected crops including cereals, oilseeds, vegetable brassicas, top fruit, legumes, soft fruit, leafy vegetables, stem vegetables, bulb vegetables, fruiting vegetables and root and tuber crops), including those grown for forage or fodder (grazing or animal feed)<br><br>↘ **Herbs**<br><br>↘ **Agricultural herbage** (any type of crop grown to feed livestock)<br><br>↘ **Edible fungi**<br><br>↘ **Apiculture** (empty honeycombs and beehives)<br><br>↘ **Other edible crops** (for example hops, figs, quinoa) | ↘ **Green cover** (grass or plants on land that is temporarily not being used to produce edible crops)<br><br>↘ **Forestry**<br><br>Forest nurseries<br><br>Forests or woodland for producing timber for sale, coppicing (broad-leaved trees like hazel or willow that can be cut down to the stump and regrow with lots of stems, called poles, which can be harvested and used in a wide range of products)<br><br>Forests or woodland for amenity, recreation, conservation and landscaping<br><br>Farm forestry on arable land or improved grassland<br><br>Cut logs and felled timber waiting to go to the saw mill<br><br>↘ **Ornamental plants**<br><br>↘ **Industrial crops** (for example, *Miscanthus* spp grown for any industrial use) | ↘ **Structural treatments**<br><br>Crop storage areas and equipment for handling crops<br><br>Protected cropping structures<br><br>Interior landscapes<br><br>↘ **Use in or near water**<br><br>Land immediately next to water<br><br>Areas of an estuary between the low- and high-tide marks<br><br>Open or enclosed water |

| Industrial and amenity areas | Plant-free areas (herbicides only) | Vertebrate control in plant protection situations |
|---|---|---|
| ⬊ **Amenity grassland** (areas of semi-natural or planted grassland that need little management, such as golf fairways, road verges and parkland)<br><br>⬊ **Amenity vegetation** (areas of semi-natural or ornamental plants, including trees and bare soil around ornamental plants)<br><br>⬊ **Managed turf** (areas of frequently mown, intensively-managed turf such as sports pitches, golf and bowling greens and tennis courts) | ⬊ **Natural surfaces that plants are not supposed to grow on** (areas of soil or natural rock such as strips around fields, fence lines and barriers, but not including land between rows of crops)<br><br>⬊ **Permeable surfaces (that is, surfaces that liquids can pass through) on top of soil** (any man-made permeable surface, such as gravel, that lies over the soil and that plants are not supposed to grow on. This includes permeable sports surfaces but not railway ballast – stones forming the bed of a railway track)<br><br>⬊ **Hard surfaces** (any man-made impermeable surface – that is, a surface that liquid cannot pass through – such as concrete or tarmac that plants should not grow on, including railway ballast)<br><br>⬊ **Wooden surfaces** (such as decking) | ⬊ **Products** for use in the situations described above (such as agricultural fields, glasshouses, forestry and amenity areas) to protect plants or plant material |

You can get more detailed information on the crop types and uses (known as the 'crop hierarchy') on the Pesticides Safety Directorate (PSD) website at: www.pesticides.gov.uk/psd_databases.asp?id=327

**IF YOU ARE PROSECUTED FOR NOT FOLLOWING THE CODE, A COURT WILL FIND YOU GUILTY UNLESS YOU CAN SHOW THAT YOU HAVE OBEYED THE LAW IN SOME OTHER WAY.**

## 1.4 WHAT IS THE LEGAL STATUS OF THIS CODE?

This code gives advice on how to use pesticides safely.

The code has a special position in law. If you follow its advice you will be doing enough to keep within the law. But you may be able to work in a different way from the code as long as that way is just as safe.

If you are prosecuted for not following the code, a court will find you guilty unless you can show that you have obeyed the law in some other way.

## 1.5 WHO SHOULD READ THIS CODE?

This code should be read by everyone who uses pesticides professionally:

↘ on farms and holdings;

↘ in horticulture;

↘ on amenity areas, industrial areas and sports grounds; and

↘ in forestry.

People who provide advice or practical support, or sell and supply pesticides, should be familiar with this code.

If you use pesticides as part of your job but not to protect plants, read the Health and Safety Commission's approved 'Code of Practice on the safe use of pesticides for non-agricultural purposes' (see **annex B**).

This code is not for people who use pesticides in their homes or as part of their gardening hobby. These people should follow the relevant product label. They can also get general advice on using pesticides from garden centres, trade organisations like the Crop Protection Association (www.cropprotection.org.uk) and from a wide range of other publications.

## 1.6 WHAT OTHER ADVICE IS AVAILABLE?

As well as the advice in this code and on product labels, you may need to read other advice issued by the Government, the industry or other organisations. That advice is referred to in the appropriate sections of this code. **Annex B** gives a list of all codes of practice, guidance notes and other advice currently available.

## 1.7 SPECIAL TERMS

The special terms used in this publication are explained in **annex C**. These terms include descriptions of methods of applying pesticides and the equipment used. You may find these helpful when deciding which certificate of competence covers a particular method of applying pesticide.

## 1.8 CROSS COMPLIANCE

In order to receive payments under the Single Farm Payment Scheme (and certain other payment support schemes) farmers and crofters have to comply with the full range of cross compliance requirements. A number of the Statutory Management Requirements relate in particular to the use of plant protection products and to record keeping. Information on cross compliance can be found on the Scottish Executive website (www.scotland. gov.uk/Topics/Agriculture/grants/Schemes/ccompliance) See also **glossary 1, annex C**.

# 2

# TRAINING AND CERTIFICATION

# BY LAW THERE ARE CERTAIN SITUATIONS WHERE YOU WILL NEED TO HAVE A QUALIFICATION CALLED A 'CERTIFICATE OF COMPETENCE'.

## 2.1 WHO MUST BE TRAINED IN USING PESTICIDES?

By law, everyone who uses pesticides professionally must have received adequate training in using pesticides safely and be skilled in the job they are carrying out. This applies to:

↘ users, operators and technicians (including contractors);

↘ managers;

↘ employers;

↘ self-employed people; and

↘ people who give instruction to others on how to use pesticides.

By law there are certain situations where you will need to have a qualification called a 'certificate of competence'. In general, you will need a certificate of competence if you supply, store or use 'agricultural pesticides'. These are pesticides used:

↘ in agriculture;

↘ in horticulture (including horticulture of amenity areas such as parks, streets, sports pitches and so on);

↘ in forestry;

↘ in or near water; and

↘ as industrial herbicides.

The circumstances in which you need a certificate of competence are explained and set out in flow diagrams later in this section.

## 2.2 WHAT TRAINING DO I NEED?

Before using a pesticide, you will need basic training in the subjects set out in **table 2** below.

**TABLE 2** Subjects you need to know about

| Subject | Why you need to know about this |
| --- | --- |
| The relevant laws | To understand and keep to the wide range of regulations on using pesticides and the legal conditions of a particular product being approved. |
| The risks associated with pesticides. (That is, whether the substance itself can harm people, wildlife or the environment.) | For you to identify whether a pesticide you are using, or intend to use, could harm people, plants and creatures you don't intend to treat, or the environment. |
| The risks which may result from using pesticides. (That is, whether the pesticide is capable of causing harm because of how it is, or will be, used.) | To assess and control the risks to people (operators, bystanders, people living near or entering treated areas and those handling or eating treated items), plants and creatures you don't intend to treat and the environment. |
| Safe working practices | So you can keep the risks to people, plants and creatures you don't intend to treat and the environment as low as possible when you are:<br><br>↘ storing, handling and mixing pesticides;<br><br>↘ making sure that the dose levels are correct (calibrating);<br><br>↘ using and cleaning equipment; and<br><br>↘ disposing of pesticide waste.<br><br>This includes reducing exposure by using engineering controls and understanding how to use and look after personal protective equipment. |
| Emergency action | For you to protect people, plants and creatures you don't intend to treat and the environment get help, and let others know, if there is a pesticide spillage, contaminated person, fire or other incident. |

| Subject | Why you need to know about this |
|---|---|
| Health monitoring | So that you (if you are self-employed) or your employer understands when to use health or exposure monitoring methods. |
| Record keeping | To make sure that you (or the person responsible for keeping records) understand which records are needed, how to make and keep them, and how to give people access to them to keep to the law. This may include records of: |
| | ↘ pesticide treatments, including any specific records needed to meet the conditions of 'local environmental risk assessment for pesticides' schemes or crop or woodland assurance schemes, as necessary; |
| | ↘ assessments under the Control of Substances Hazardous to Health (COSHH) Regulations 2002; |
| | ↘ inspection and maintenance records for engineering controls and respiratory protective equipment; and |
| | ↘ monitoring health and exposure levels. |
| Using equipment for applying pesticide | To make sure you can work all equipment you need to use safely and effectively and have had further training for specific techniques or activities (for example, reduced volume spraying or applying pesticides in or near water). |

# THE TYPE OF CERTIFICATE NEEDED WILL DEPEND ON THE PRODUCT YOU ARE USING AND YOUR INDIVIDUAL CIRCUMSTANCES.

## 2.3 WHEN WOULD I NEED A CERTIFICATE OF COMPETENCE?

Although everyone who uses pesticides professionally must be trained, in some situations the law states that users must have an appropriate certificate of competence. The type of certificate needed will depend on the product you are using and your individual circumstances.

Use the following flow charts to see if you need a certificate of competence.

**FLOW CHART 1:** Is a certificate needed for the product I plan to use?

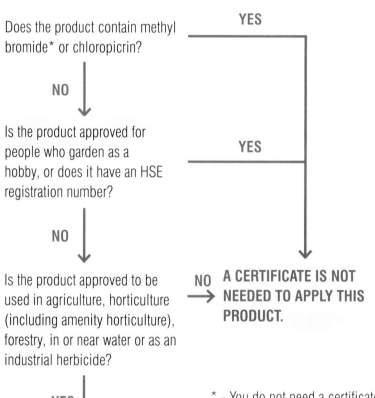

Does the product contain methyl bromide* or chloropicrin?

**YES**

**NO**

Is the product approved for people who garden as a hobby, or does it have an HSE registration number?

**YES**

**NO**

Is the product approved to be used in agriculture, horticulture (including amenity horticulture), forestry, in or near water or as an industrial herbicide?

**NO** → **A CERTIFICATE IS NOT NEEDED TO APPLY THIS PRODUCT.**

**YES**

**A CERTIFICATE IS NEEDED – GO TO THE NEXT FLOW DIAGRAM TO SEE IF YOU PERSONALLY NEED TO GET ONE.**

\* - You do not need a certificate under pesticide and plant protection product laws but you should note that the Ozone Depleting Substances (Qualifications) Regulations will be coming into force in 2006 which make a certificate from the British Pest Control Association a necessity.

**FLOW CHART 2**: Do I need a certificate?

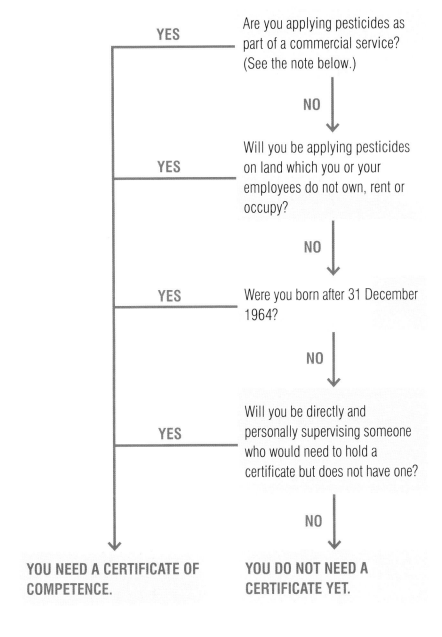

**YES**

Are you applying pesticides as part of a commercial service? (See the note below.)

**NO** ↓

**YES**

Will you be applying pesticides on land which you or your employees do not own, rent or occupy?

**NO** ↓

**YES**

Were you born after 31 December 1964?

**NO** ↓

**YES**

Will you be directly and personally supervising someone who would need to hold a certificate but does not have one?

**NO** ↓

**YOU NEED A CERTIFICATE OF COMPETENCE.**

**YOU DO NOT NEED A CERTIFICATE YET.**

**NOTE:** You are supplying a commercial service if:

↘ the crops, land, produce, materials, buildings or the contents of buildings you are treating are not owned, occupied or rented by you or your employer; or

↘ you are applying pesticide to seed that will be used on land not owned, occupied or rented by you or your employer, even if the pesticide is provided by the land owner.

## 2.4 HOW CAN I USE PESTICIDES WITHOUT A CERTIFICATE OF COMPETENCE?

If you need to have a certificate of competence to do your job, but you do not have one yet, you must be supervised by a person who has the necessary certificate.

If you are supervising someone who does not have a certificate, you should be able to see and hear the person doing the job to supervise them. You should be able to see the person doing all parts of the job, including:

↘ preparing and mixing the pesticide;

↘ filling equipment and making sure the dose levels are correct (calibrating);

↘ applying the pesticide; and

↘ cleaning equipment and disposing of washings, leftover pesticides and the containers.

Always look out for changes in the law and remember that you need to be trained and skilled in what you do. Make sure your knowledge is up to date. Even if you do not need a certificate of competence, you might like to get one as proof of your experience, knowledge and skills.

**ALWAYS LOOK OUT FOR CHANGES IN THE LAW AND REMEMBER THAT YOU NEED TO BE TRAINED AND SKILLED IN WHAT YOU DO.**

2

## 2.5 WHERE DO I GET CERTIFICATES OF COMPETENCE?

If you use 'agricultural pesticides' in Scotland (as explained in the introduction section of this code), get in touch with the Scottish Skills Testing Service (SSTS) (contact details are given in **annex D**). The SSTS is the main NPTC assessment centre in Scotland. If you use fumigants, get in touch with the British Pest Control Association (contact details are given in **annex D**).

You will need to arrange any training you need, and pass your tests. Training for NPTC certificates of competence is provided by many agricultural colleges, independent training providers and trade associations. Training in using fumigants and vertebrate control agents is provided through the British Pest Control Association (BPCA) and by the NPTC. You can get a list of registered local training providers and details of other relevant qualifications which meet the National Occupational Standard from Lantra Sector Skills Council (the national training organisation for land-based industries).

You can get training for the BASIS Certificate in Crop Protection from some agricultural colleges and independent training providers. You can get more information from BASIS (Registration) Limited (contact details are given in **annex D**).

If your employer provides their own training, it needs to be equivalent to the standards described above.

If you want an NPTC certificate of competence you generally need to successfully complete a foundation unit before taking other units that are appropriate for the type of equipment you are using or the type of work you are doing. You should get advice from the SSTS if you are not sure which certificate of competence you need for any particular use. A list of the types of equipment and methods covered by the various NPTC units is given in **glossary 2** in **annex C**.

For some types of pesticide you do not need a certificate of competence, but you must have been given adequate and relevant training. (For example, you do not necessarily need a certificate of competence to use vertebrate control agents - products used to control small animals such as, rodenticides - even though relevant certificates are available from the BPCA and the NPTC.). However, you must have received appropriate training before using the pesticide. If you use products that release gas (such as phosphine-generating products), by law you must have had specific training in using these products.

Once you have the appropriate certificate of competence you do not need to renew that certificate in the future. But you should make sure you keep your skills, knowledge and training up to date. You should always have the latest information. You may need to develop further technical knowledge or practical skills as technology changes. This is called continuing professional development (CPD). Trade associations, the SSTS, the BPCA and other vocational organisations will be able to help you with this. Remember that everyone who works with pesticides must make sure that they protect the health of people, other creatures and plants, protect the environment, and avoid polluting water.

You should keep a record of all the training you receive. It is the easiest way for you to prove that you have the necessary training, knowledge and skills. Also, some contracts and agreements may make it a condition that pesticides are only applied by certificated operators.

## 2.6 WHAT TRAINING AND CERTIFICATES ARE NEEDED FOR SALESPEOPLE, ADVISERS, MANAGERS AND PEOPLE WHO DRAFT CONTRACTS?

**EVEN IF YOU HAVE A CERTIFICATE OF COMPETENCE OR EVIDENCE OF OTHER TRAINING, IT IS IMPORTANT THAT YOU DEVELOP YOUR TECHNICAL KNOWLEDGE AND PRACTICAL SKILLS IN USING PESTICIDES.**

By law, everyone who sells pesticides for agricultural use must have a certificate of competence or be working under the direct supervision of someone with a certificate of competence. You should contact BASIS (Registration) Ltd to find out about this type of course. If you sell pesticides you should make sure that you are familiar with the Code of Practice for Suppliers of Pesticides to Agriculture, Horticulture and Forestry (the yellow code).

Although the NPTC foundation unit is not recognised on its own as a certificate of competence, it is a useful qualification for people responsible for working with pesticides but who do not apply them themselves. Other qualifications that are not needed by law are available specifically for people who make policy and operational decisions about applying pesticides and these may be useful for managers and supervisors. You should be sure that the person you ask for advice has the necessary skills, knowledge and experience. Also, people who draft contracts should have suitable training and experience to do so, even though they do not need to have a certificate of competence to do their job. You can get further information from BASIS, SSTS and Lantra Awards (contact information is given in **annex D**).

Further courses are offered by SSTS, BASIS, Lantra Sector Skills Council and other organisations. These courses are vocational and are not needed by law.

## 2.7 CONTINUING PROFESSIONAL DEVELOPMENT (CPD)

Even if you have a certificate of competence or evidence of other training, it is important that you develop your technical knowledge and practical skills in using pesticides. Whether you need a certificate of competence or not, you should make sure that you keep your training up to date and that you know the latest information on how to protect human health, wildlife, other plants and creatures you don't intend to treat, water and the environment.

You can get evidence of your continuing professional development by being a member of:

↘ the National Register of Sprayer Operators (if you use pesticides); and

↘ the BASIS Professional Register (if you sell or supply pesticides).

You will need the appropriate certificates of competence to join these schemes (unless you want to join the National Register of Sprayer Operators and were born before 1 January 1965). To continue to be a member, you will need to go to appropriate training events and conferences, in line with the terms of each scheme.

3

# PLANNING AND PREPARATION

## 3.1 MAKING THE RISK OF USING PESTICIDES AS LOW AS POSSIBLE

This part of the code provides guidance on what you need to consider before using a pesticide to make sure that you apply it in a way that is safe and effective and meets the relevant laws.

### 3.1.1 CONSIDERING WHETHER TO USE A PESTICIDE

It is Government policy to keep pesticide use to the lowest possible level while making sure that pests, diseases and weeds are effectively controlled in a way which protects the health of people, and safeguards biodiversity, which means, other creatures (including beneficial insects), plants and the environment. All public bodies in the course of their functions have a duty, under the Nature Conservation (Scotland) Act 2004, to further biodiversity, so far as it is consistent with the proper exercise of those functions. Always consider whether you need to use a pesticide, including pesticide-treated seed, at all. In many situations you may be able to prevent or limit pest, disease and weed problems by following good practices. For example, you may use appropriate crop rotations, different varieties of crop, cultivation methods, fertilisers and so on.

It is important to tackle a problem as soon as you identify it but before you use a pesticide you should consider whether you could tackle the problem better in other ways (for example, by using cultural or biological control methods or a combination of these methods with pesticides, in line with the principles of 'integrated crop management' and 'integrated pest management').

*The Defra booklet 'Pesticides and integrated farm management' gives more guidance on integrated crop management and integrated pest management. You can also get more information from Linking Environment and Farming (contact details in annex D).*

## ALWAYS USE A PRODUCT IN LINE WITH ITS APPROVED CONDITIONS OF USE.

An appropriate computer-based system may help you to consider all of the relevant factors before you use a pesticide. You may also find it helpful to use one of the laboratory tests or in-field test kits available to identify a range of crop diseases, or a trap to help monitor insect pests. These methods may help you to decide whether you need to use a pesticide, which one to use, and the best time to use it.

Using pesticides when you don't need to is not just a waste of money, it can also contribute to pests building up a resistance to products which then become less effective in the future. You should always:

↘ use a pesticide in a carefully planned way;

↘ know the principles of using pesticides over the long term; and

↘ consider the long-term implications whenever you use a pesticide.

### 3.1.2 WHAT TO DO IF YOU DECIDE THAT YOU NEED TO USE A PESTICIDE

If, after considering all the alternatives, you decide that you need to use a pesticide, there are still a number of ways in which you can keep any unwanted effects of a pesticide as low as possible.

↘ For the pesticide to be as effective as possible it is essential that you use the correct product at the right time and in the right way.

↘ Always use a product in line with its approved conditions of use. Always consider if you can use a dose which is lower than the maximum dose allowed by the product label. You should think carefully about whether lowering the dose might have an effect on managing pesticide resistance. You may need to get professional advice to decide on the appropriate dose for your situation.

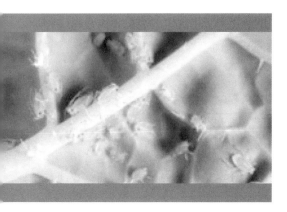

 **IT IS ESSENTIAL THAT YOU CHOOSE THE RIGHT PRODUCT IN EACH SITUATION.**

In some situations, you may be able to apply the lowest possible amount of pesticide by better targeting. For example, by:

➘ applying the product as a spot, patch or varied-dose treatment, possibly using GPS (global positioning system) mapping techniques or optical sensing of weeds on hard surfaces; or

➘ using 'weed wipers' to apply some herbicides in grassland and similar situations, if the approved conditions of use allow this, to treat only the relevant vegetation.

In all situations, consider the effects the product could have on people's health and the environment. The COSHH assessment and assessment of risks to the environment may confirm that the pesticide you have chosen is the most appropriate. However, if you find that using another suitable pesticide may involve less risk to people's health or the environment, or is likely to lead to a lower risk of resistance, you will need to consider your choice again.

A range of pests, weeds and diseases have built up resistance to certain pesticides which were once effective. It is important that pesticides are used in a way which reduces the build-up of resistance so the pesticides that are currently available remain effective. To do this you should:

➘ use all pesticides as part of a strategy of managing resistance;

➘ include non-chemical methods of pest, weed and disease control;

➘ consider, where appropriate, future crop rotation, and not just the current crop; and

➘ monitor the effectiveness of pesticide treatments and note any potential resistance problems.

# IN ALL SITUATIONS, CONSIDER THE EFFECTS THAT THE PRODUCT COULD HAVE ON PEOPLE'S HEALTH AND THE ENVIRONMENT.

*You can get information on pesticide resistance and the work of the various resistance action groups (RAGs) dealing with fungicides (FRAG), weeds (WRAG), insecticides (IRAG) and rodenticides (RRAG) on the PSD website (www.pesticides.gov.uk/rags_home. asp). You can also get advice on resistance management from some product labels and from advisers and pesticide manufacturers.*

### 3.1.3 CHOOSING THE RIGHT PESTICIDE

It is essential that you choose the right product in each situation. You may find it helpful to use a computer-based system to help you find the right product. If you are not qualified to choose the most appropriate pesticide, you should consult a suitably qualified adviser who will also be able to tell you when and how to use the pesticide and what dose to apply.

When discussing your pesticide needs with a supplier, distributor or adviser, check whether the product:

↘ is currently approved for the intended use and situation;

↘ can be safely prepared and applied using the intended equipment;

↘ can be used in line with any harvest interval, access restriction for workers or livestock, or application restriction (for instance, a buffer zone) shown on the product label;

↘ presents the least risk to the health of people (you and people entering or living near treated areas) in comparison to other suitable pesticides;

↘ presents the least overall risk to livestock, the environment (including surface water and groundwater) and other creatures; (including other biological control agents); and

↘ fits in with your strategy for managing resistance.

PREPARATION

## 3.2 THE PRODUCT LABEL

### 3.2.1 EXPLANATION

The main source of information that helps you to use a pesticide safely and effectively is the product label. This must come with the product container at the time you are supplied with the product. The label is normally permanently fixed to the container but, for some products, detachable or separate leaflets will be supplied.

### 3.2.2 OTHER INFORMATION

Other relevant information may come from your supplier and can include the following.

↘ Material safety data sheets (MSDS). These have important information on what to do in an emergency though this information often also appears on the product label for many products.

↘ For many amenity products, information cards that can be given to members of the public who ask about the product; and

↘ Environmental information sheets (EIS) are available for many products to add to the information on the product label about the risks to the environment and how to control them.

You may want to check the Voluntary Initiative website (www.voluntaryinitiative.org.uk) to see what information you can find.

### 3.2.3 CHECKING THE APPROVAL

You cannot assume that a product you have used before is still approved as a suitable product or for a particular use. This is because product approvals are frequently changed. You must especially check approvals for commodity substances (see **glossary 1** in **annex C**), off-label uses or imported pesticides identical to products already approved in the UK. These approvals are the best information available on using the product.

If you are not sure, up-to-date information on approval status is available on the PSD website (www.pesticides.gov.uk).

You should check for the UK approval status of any foreign pesticide before you buy it. Unless the product is approved in the UK you will be committing an offence if you store and use a foreign product, even if there is a label written in English.

**YOU CANNOT ASSUME THAT A PRODUCT YOU HAVE USED BEFORE IS STILL APPROVED AS A SUITABLE PRODUCT OR FOR A PARTICULAR USE.**

PREPARATION

### 3.2.4 THE LABEL

All labels have the phrase 'Read all safety precautions and directions for use before use'. It is essential that you read and understand all the information contained in the label (and any leaflets supplied with the product). Only by doing so will you be able to use the pesticide safely and effectively, taking account of the specific proposed treatment and the circumstances and environmental conditions. By law you must take 'all reasonable precautions' when using pesticides. To do this you must consider the label as a whole and make a judgement about the equipment and how you intend to use the product.

When reading a product label, the most important parts to consider are protecting you, protecting the environment, protecting consumers, storage and disposal, and medical advice. Some of these factors on the label will apply to more than one of these groups.

a.  Protecting you and others around you – check whether the label says anything about:

↘ the need to carry out a COSHH assessment, as appropriate;

↘ the need to use engineering controls (for example, closed cabs when making air-assisted applications);

↘ the need to use specific personal protective equipment (PPE);

↘ any medical conditions which may be made worse (for example, when intending to use a product containing an organophosphate or a carbamate with anticholinesterase effects – see glossary 1 in annex C);

↘ the need for treated areas to be ventilated after treatment before re-entry and/or entry to be prevented for set periods of time; and

↘ other safety measures such as:

-   cleaning the PPE;

-   what to do if someone is contaminated;

-   the need for any specialised training;

-   good hygiene practice; and

-   using refillable containers.

b. Protecting the environment – check whether the label says anything about:

↘ not using the product outside;

↘ the need for keeping the areas out of bounds after treatment to protect livestock;

↘ removing or burying spillages;

↘ the need for buffer zones to protect water, and whether they can be reduced by LERAP assessments;

↘ the need for buffer zones to protect insects and other creatures you don't intend to treat;

↘ the need to remove pets and livestock before use or to keep animals and birds out of the treatment area; and

↘ protecting bees by not treating flowering plants.

c. Protecting consumers – check whether the label says anything about:

↘ not using the product on food crops, in food storage or preparation areas or in occupied buildings;

↘ the maximum dose or maximum concentration for some products applied as high-volume sprays;

↘ the maximum number of treatments or maximum total dose;

↘ the latest time that the product can be used depending on the crop-growth stage or harvest interval; and

↘ other specific restrictions (for example, the maximum concentration of the product in the spray solution or the minimum water volume, the minimum interval between applications or restrictions on using certain types of equipment to apply the product).

d. Storage and disposal – check whether the label says anything about:

↘ storing the product away from food, drink, animal feed and where children cannot see or reach it;

↘ keeping products locked away;

↘ storing products that are supplied in water soluble sachets; and

↘ rinsing, emptying, disposing of, returning or reusing the container type (as appropriate).

e. Medical advice – check whether the label says anything about:

↘ what to do if someone is contaminated or suffers health problems after using pesticides;

↘ contacting the National Poisons Information Service (NPIS); and

↘ other types of first aid.

# IF YOU ARE APPLYING A PESTICIDE THAT HAS BEEN MIXED BY ANOTHER PERSON, YOU MUST HAVE READ AND UNDERSTOOD THE PRODUCT LABEL AND SHOULD HAVE A COPY AVAILABLE.

### 3.2.5 OFF-LABEL APPROVALS

You (or organisations representing pesticide users) may apply for a 'specific off-label approval' (SOLA) for a product which is already approved for other uses. Off-label approval details are not given in the information provided by pesticide manufacturers (for example, the product label or leaflets). You must use a pesticide product in line with its SOLA, the product label and leaflet and any extra guidance on off-label approvals. This means you must read, understand and follow the Notice of Approval. You can find these notices on the PSD website (www.pesticides.gov.uk).

If you choose to use a pesticide in line with a SOLA, you are responsible for the risk to your business.

### 3.2.6 TREATED SEEDS, CUTTINGS AND SO ON

The labelling of treated seed and treated plant propagating material (seedlings, cuttings and so on) is not covered by pesticide laws. However, voluntary labelling guidelines have been agreed to make sure that appropriate safety information is provided with these types of material.

### 3.2.7 APPLYING A PRE-PREPARED PESTICIDE

If you are applying a pesticide which has been mixed by another person (for example, a spray solution or prepared bait), you must have read and understood the product label and should have a copy available.

*For more information on the labelling of pesticide products, see 'The Labelling Handbook' available on the PSD website (www.pesticides.gov.uk).*

PREPARATION

## 3.3 STORING PESTICIDES

### 3.3.1 INFORMATION SOURCE

You can get detailed guidance on how you can store pesticides safely and legally from the Health and Safety Executive (HSE). The HSE's agriculture information sheet number 16 sets out the appropriate standards for fixed and mobile stores. It explains the extra precautions which you need to take when storing particularly dangerous pesticides (such as gassing compounds and oxidising agents). You should read this information sheet before building a new store, moving a store, converting an existing building or structure, using a storage cabinet or using a mobile store. You can download a copy of this from the HSE website (www.hse.gov.uk/pubns/ais16.pdf).

### 3.3.2 HOW SHOULD I STORE PESTICIDES?

You must only store approved pesticides in the original container with the approved product label. The procedure for dealing with leaking containers is described in the emergency procedures clauses at the beginning of this book.

When you have mixed a pesticide with another substance (such as a diluent, carrier, marker or adjuvant), you are strongly recommended to use the mixture as soon as possible and not to store it for a long period. You should only have enough mixture to use in a day. If, due to unforeseen circumstances, you need to store a mixture for longer than this, you will need to make sure that it is labelled properly and stored safely and securely.

If you are storing professional pesticides which you sell or supply to others, further storage conditions are likely to apply. Also, if you are storing over 200 kilograms or 200 litres of professional pesticides which you will sell or supply to others, you will need storekeeper training and certificates. These obligations are explained in the Defra 'Code of practice for suppliers of pesticides to agriculture, horticulture and forestry' (the yellow code).

Make sure that your store has suitable equipment for dealing with contamination, spills and small fires, and that you know how to use the equipment. You should also have a list of appropriate emergency phone numbers clearly displayed.

Practise good store management by making sure that you:

↘ do not have unapproved or unwanted pesticides in your store;

↘ remove waste packaging and dispose of it safely and legally;

↘ use the oldest stock first;

↘ deal with damaged or deteriorating containers; and

↘ have an up-to-date stock record easily available and, in case of emergency, keep a copy away from the store for safekeeping.

3

# YOU MUST ONLY STORE APPROVED PESTICIDES IN THE ORIGINAL CONTAINER WITH THE APPROVED PRODUCT LABEL.

# YOU SHOULD NEVER CARRY PESTICIDES IN THE CAB OF A TRACTOR, SELF-PROPELLED EQUIPMENT OR OTHER VEHICLE.

### 3.3.3 WHAT EXTRA CONDITIONS APPLY TO MOBILE STORES?

You should make sure that all pesticides are safely transported to where they will be applied and stay safely stored at the site.

When you store pesticides in vehicles, in bowsers (storage tanks, sometimes moveable) or on equipment used to apply the pesticide, these mobile stores should be:

↘ stocked from a fixed store; and

↘ used temporarily (normally for less than 24 hours).

If you need to use mobile storage for longer than 24 hours (for example, if you are a contractor routinely involved in large tasks away from your base), you should make sure that your store meets the higher standards set for fixed stores.

You should never carry pesticides in the cab of a tractor, self-propelled equipment or other vehicle. Use either:

↘ a vehicle with a bulkhead between the cab and the load compartment (check that the load-carrying area has nothing which might damage containers);

↘ a secure enclosed chemical container; or

↘ a secure cabinet mounted on the outside of the vehicle or on a trailer.

Gassing compounds should be stored in a separate vapour-proof container which is secured within the load compartment.

You should park your mobile store away from places where a spill would be likely to cause water pollution. Make sure that you lock the vehicle or cabinet whenever you are not around.

If you transport pesticides marked 'Toxic', 'Flammable', or 'Corrosive', you may have extra legal responsibilities, particularly if you are transporting more than 200 litres or 200 kilograms. These extra responsibilities may also apply to smaller quantities of very dangerous substances such as gassing compounds.

*You can find detailed information on how to act in line with the law when transporting pesticides in a mobile store in 'The carriage of agrochemicals by road: Guidance for the agrochemicals industry' available from BASIS (Registration) Ltd.*

PREPARATION

# DEAL WITH ANY SPILLAGE IMMEDIATELY AND DISPOSE OF ALL CONTAMINATED MATERIAL SAFELY AND LEGALLY.

### 3.3.4 MOVING PESTICIDES INTO, AND OUT OF, THE STORE

You should move containers in and out of the store carefully, particularly if you think that they may have deteriorated or been damaged. Before you move containers, check that they are not leaking, that they are securely closed and that the label (including associated information) is intact and can be read.

Deal with any spillage immediately and dispose of all contaminated material safely and legally.

### 3.3.5 DO NOT LEAVE PESTICIDE CONTAINERS UNATTENDED

When pesticides are not in a secure store, you must not leave them unattended or where the person in charge of them can't see them. Stolen pesticides may be misused, causing harm to people and the environment. Unattended pesticides are a risk to people (especially children), pets, working animals, livestock and wildlife. For example, a dog can eat through the unopened packaging of slug pellets. A fully trained person should be present when pesticides are being moved or transported, and all deliveries should be supervised to make sure that stocks are stored safely and securely.

## 3.4 THE COSHH ASSESSMENT

*The Health and Safety Executive (HSE) publishes free information and guidance on how to carry out a COSHH assessment, such as 'A step by step guide to COSHH assessment'. You can get this from your local HSE office or from the HSE website (www.hse.gov.uk/ coshh/index.htm). You can also get further information through the HSE Info line (phone: 0845 3450055, fax: 0845 4089566, e-mail: hse.infoline@natbrit.com).*

### 3.4.1 WHEN DO COSHH REGULATIONS APPLY?

Many pesticides are dangerous to health. In these regulations, the danger is explained in terms of the 'hazard' and the 'risk'. A substance is hazardous if it could harm people, plants and creatures not being treated, or the environment. The risk from a substance is the chance of it causing harm, given the way in which it is, or will be, used.

The COSHH regulations (see **annex A**) apply to a pesticide product if it:

↘ is classified as 'very toxic', 'toxic', 'harmful', 'irritant' or 'corrosive';

↘ includes a substance which has a 'workplace exposure limit' (WEL) under the COSHH Regulations (see Health and Safety Executive (HSE) guidance note EH40);

↘ includes a micro-organism which may be a danger to health;

↘ includes dust which may be present in a 'substantial concentration' in the air (as explained in the Health and Safety Commission 'General approved code of practice on the COSHH Regulations', COP 29) when the pesticide is used; or

↘ includes any substance not mentioned above which creates a similar danger to health.

Such products will have the following phrase on the container label: 'The Control of Substances Hazardous to Health (COSHH) Regulations may apply to the use of this product at work'.

Under the COSHH regulations, before a pesticide is used an employer or self-employed person must carry out a suitable and sufficient assessment of the likely risks to health. This will help you to identify the measures that you need to take to protect the health of any person who could be harmed.

PREPARATION

### **3.4.2** WHEN IS AN ASSESSMENT SUITABLE AND SUFFICIENT?

A COSHH assessment will be suitable and sufficient if you use a well-thought-out approach to identifying risks by:

- considering the dangers posed by the pesticide you intend to use;
- deciding who could be harmed and how;
- identifying what action you need to take to prevent or control exposure;
- recording the results of the assessment; and
- revising the assessment when necessary.

The level of detail needed in the COSHH assessment will depend on the activities you are carrying out and the level of risk involved in your work.

### **3.4.3** FINDING OUT ABOUT THE DANGERS

The danger a product poses depends on the nature and concentration of the product's active ingredients and the other ingredients (co-formulants), and its form (for example, whether it is a liquid, granule, powder, gas or other type of product).

Most information on the dangers associated with a pesticide is on the product label, which will show:

- the hazard classification (for example, 'Irritant');
- the risk and safety phrases (for example, 'Irritating to eyes' and 'Wear eye protection...');
- any restrictions relating to who should use the product (for example, certain people may have been advised not to work with anticholinesterase compounds – see **glossary 1** in **annex C**); and
- other safety-related restrictions and conditions.

Other information on dangers is given in:

- information provided by the pesticide's manufacturer or supplier (for example, the material safety data sheet (MSDS), also known as the product hazard data sheet or material hazard data sheet (MHDS);
- the schedules to the COSHH regulations (see the HSC 'General approved code of practice on the COSHH Regulations', COP 29 for more information) and HSE's publication EH 40: 'Occupational exposure limits' (this sets out the acceptable levels for exposure by breathing which apply to some active ingredients used in pesticides);
- other relevant guidance material on using pesticides published by HSC, HSE, Defra, PSD and other authorities; and
- technical, scientific or legal information in relevant trade and professional publications. Use any of your own previous experience of work with the pesticides.

### 3.4.4 ASSESSING THE RISKS, WHO MIGHT BE HARMED AND HOW?

Employers or self-employed people need to consider whether any person might be at risk from being exposed to pesticides. In doing so, they need to bear in mind how and where the product will be applied, how long it will be used for, how containers will be handled, and the possibility of an accident. Talking with workers' safety representatives, if your business has them, will help you to identify risks from particular working practices.

Remember to consider:

↘ your employees (even those not using the pesticide);

↘ other people on the premises;

↘ anyone else in, or near, the area where the pesticide is used; and

↘ anyone likely to enter treated areas or be in contact with treated materials after the pesticide has been applied.

Assessing how employees and other people might be affected will mean using the information printed on the product label and applying it to the circumstances of the work to be carried out. In particular you should consider the following:

↘ Who could be exposed and how (through the skin or by breathing in or swallowing the pesticide):

-   Absorption through the skin from handling the concentrate or contaminated equipment, and from exposure to spray drift, is likely to be the main route of exposure for most pesticides.

-   Breathing in a pesticide, especially with active ingredients that arc volatile (that is, evaporate quickly at normal temperatures) and from approved indoor uses.

-   Swallowing a pesticide (possibly from hand-to-mouth or object-to-mouth).

↘ Whether the types of contamination listed above may also affect people entering treated areas or handling treated material.

↘ The extent of the exposure and what could happen if the control measures fail.

↘ What harmful effects the pesticide can have through the most likely routes into the body.

PREPARATION

# THE COSHH ASSESSMENT WILL ALSO NEED TO TAKE ACCOUNT OF ANY RISKS TO PEOPLE WHO ENTER TREATED AREAS OR HANDLE TREATED MATERIALS.

### 3.4.5 DECIDING WHAT NEEDS TO BE DONE TO CONTROL EXPOSURE

The next stage in the assessment is to identify which control measures are needed, and decide how to put these into practice, and then properly maintain them. As an employer or self-employed person, you will need to consider whether you and your employees:

↘ are suitably and sufficiently trained in using pesticides safely and using engineering control systems and PPE (see **table 2**) correctly;

↘ manage the risks associated with the hazards;

↘ understand the information on the product label and on any relevant data sheets;

↘ have suitable equipment to handle, mix, load and apply the pesticide safely;

↘ have systems or equipment (including PPE) which will prevent or, where this is not reasonably practical, adequately control, exposure;

↘ can take effective action if equipment fails or breaks down; and

↘ know the sort of ill-health effects that could be linked to being exposed to pesticides and what signs or symptoms to look out for.

The COSHH assessment will also need to take account of any risks to people who enter treated areas or handle treated materials. This will include, for example:

↘ nursery workers entering treated glasshouses after fogging or misting operations;

↘ members of the public using treated pavements or using treated land (such as sports turf and parks) for recreational purposes;

↘ forestry and nursery workers handling treated seeds, seedlings, cuttings and so on;

↘ farmers, crofters and growers handling and drilling treated seed, tubers, bulbs, onion sets and so on;

↘ people handling treated crops when harvesting, pruning or packing them;

↘ workers handling treated compost, soil and so on; and

↘ people handling freshly treated material during dipping or drenching operations.

It is good practice to give appropriate details of pesticide treatments to people who would otherwise not know about them (like members of the public and, in some cases, workers handling treated crops). Nevertheless, your COSHH assessment should assume these people will not know that a pesticide has been used and so will not know about any precautions they need to take.

Remember that you should give people enough information for them to do their work properly and be safe.

When you have completed your COSHH assessment, you will need to consider the best way to protect anyone who might be exposed to pesticides by preventing the exposure or adequately controlling it.

### 3.4.6 RECORDING THE ASSESSMENT

Where you employ 5 or more staff, you must record assessments except where the results can be explained easily and at any time. You should tell employees (or their representatives) the results of the assessment, especially the parts relating to any work they have to do.

### 3.4.7 REVIEWING THE ASSESSMENT

Under the COSHH regulations, you must review the assessment regularly. The COSHH assessment should state when you will review it. The period between reviews will depend on the risk, the type of work and the likelihood of anything changing. In any case, you should review the assessment at least every five years.

You must carry out a review straight away if you think that the assessment is no longer valid or if there has been a significant change in the work the assessment relates to. For example, what the pesticide is used for or how it is applied may change. This may arise from discussions with safety representatives or workers. An assessment may also stop being valid because of, for example, changes in the conditions of the product approval or the results of health monitoring.

***Get advice from PSD (contact details are in annex D) your supplier or the manufacturer if you think the conditions of a pesticide approval may have changed.***

PREPARATION

**THE HSE PUBLISHES GUIDANCE ON HOW TO ACT IN LINE WITH 'THE PERSONAL PROTECTIVE EQUIPMENT AT WORK REGULATIONS 1992'.**

## 3.5 PREVENTING PEOPLE BEING EXPOSED TO PESTICIDES AT WORK

### 3.5.1 COSHH

Under the COSHH regulations, if anyone (including members of the public) could be affected by a work activity involving dangerous substances, you must prevent them from being exposed to the substance or, if this is not reasonably possible, adequately control the exposure.

### 3.5.2 HOW CAN EXPOSURE BE PREVENTED OR ADEQUATELY CONTROLLED?

Preventing or adequately controlling exposure involves a combination of measures. In order of priority, these are:

↘ preventing exposure (for example, by using a different product);

↘ technical, engineering or operational controls; and

↘ personal protective equipment (PPE).

*The HSE publication 'COSHH Essentials' gives guidance on control measures for processes such as transferring, weighing and mixing chemicals. You can get more information from the COSHH website (www.coshh-essentials.org.uk ).*

Under the COSHH regulations, it is better to use engineering or other control measures rather than PPE. The main concern is to create a safe working environment rather than to protect a person working in contaminated conditions. However, in the case of pesticides, people will usually need PPE as well as engineering or other controls in order to adequately control exposure. Even if the COSHH regulations do not apply, employers may still have duties under other laws, such as those relating to using protective equipment at work (see **annex A**).

*The HSE publishes guidance on how to act in line with 'The Personal Protective Equipment at Work Regulations 1992'.*

When considering how to prevent or control exposure to people entering treated areas or handling treated materials, remember that, in many situations, these people will not know what pesticides have been used or what precautions they need to take. You should use appropriate controls in these situations.

### 3.5.3 MEASURES FOR PREVENTING EXPOSURE TO PESTICIDES

You can prevent exposure to pesticides in the following ways:

⬊ By using another method of pest control;

⬊ By using a pesticide that is less dangerous, or using a less dangerous form of the same pesticide. For example, you could use a product supplied in water-soluble bags to avoid handling and measuring the product; and

⬊ By organising the work to keep non-essential people away from the areas that are being treated. For example, you could use remote-controlled equipment to apply pesticides in glasshouses.

### 3.5.4 MEASURES FOR CONTROLLING EXPOSURE TO PESTICIDES

To control exposure when you are preparing a pesticide (for example, when opening containers and transferring, diluting, mixing or loading the product), you should do the following:

⬊ Buy pesticides in a pack size to suit the area you can treat at one time or to suit the volume of spray solution being prepared. In this way you can avoid having to weigh or measure the correct dose for each load;

⬊ Use products supplied in water-soluble bags;

⬊ Use closed-transfer systems (something designed and manufactured to be used to move agricultural chemicals from their original container into a sprayer tank, and to accurately measure the volume of chemical being transferred) with compatible packaging;

⬊ Use pressure-rinsing devices to avoid rinsing containers by hand; and

⬊ Follow the good practice described in this code.

To control exposure to pesticides when you are using them, handling equipment, dealing with spillages or disposing of any pesticide wastes, you should do the following:

⬊ Reduce the dose of the product whenever this is appropriate;

⬊ Choose the right equipment for the job, such as using automatic or remote-controlled equipment for treating crops in glasshouses. If the application method you plan to use is likely to increase the risks to users, consider using another method of applying the product or controlling the pest;

⬊ Wherever possible, use a closed cab on a tractor, other vehicle or application equipment. This is especially important for application methods involving a high risk to users of contamination, such as when using air-assisted equipment; and

⬊ You should consider having your sprayer tested in line with best practice;

*The National Sprayer Testing Scheme (NSTS), run by the Agricultural Engineers Association (AEA), is an independent voluntary inspection and testing scheme for a variety of equipment used to apply pesticides. A valid test certificate provides evidence to customers, assurance schemes and the general public that application equipment is working correctly. You can find more information on the NSTS website at www.nsts.org.uk*

⬊ Make sure new equipment meets appropriate standards and is designed to keep the risk of contamination during use or maintenance as low as possible. This may include using equipment with in-cab controls for major functions, self-flushing filters, hydraulically-operated boom folding and built-in tank-washing systems and so on;

PREPARATION

# KEEP ALL EQUIPMENT WELL MAINTAINED AND DO NOT USE FAULTY EQUIPMENT;

↘ Consider fitting remote controls to equipment. Don't put them in places where they could be contaminated. They may be put in the cab where appropriate, but you should avoid routing hoses through the cab;

↘ Make sure nozzles are in good condition and do not drip when the sprayer is switched off. Check valves and associated pressure-relief systems and so on;

↘ Where possible, cover nozzles, other atomisers and powder dispensers, especially for hand-held equipment and equipment used near workers;

↘ Keep equipment that applies pesticide clean, both inside and out, using appropriate cleaning methods. When cleaning dusty or dry deposits, do not use air lines or dry brushing as these methods can lead to contamination getting into the air;

↘ Keep all equipment well maintained and do not use faulty equipment;

*The Scottish Executive booklet 'Is your sprayer fit for work?' provides guidance on maintaining and checking field crop sprayers (see annex B).*

↘ Calibrate (check the accuracy of the dose rate) in spraying equipment without using a pesticide. For products applied as granules, use the manufacturer's dummy formulations or other materials available; and

↘ Follow the good practice described in this code.

*To make sure that your equipment is working as it should be and is accurate, read the manufacturer's instructions. You can find further useful information in the BCPC publications 'Boom and Fruit Sprayers Handbook' and 'Hand-Held and Amenity Sprayers Handbook' (see annex B).*

3

# EVEN WHEN THE PRODUCT LABEL OR RELEVANT NOTICE OF APPROVAL DOES NOT REFER TO PPE, IT IS GOOD PRACTICE TO WEAR BASIC PPE WHEN HANDLING AND APPLYING PESTICIDES.

### 3.5.5 USING PERSONAL PROTECTIVE EQUIPMENT (PPE)

You must wear PPE if other controls are not reasonably practical, or may not give the necessary level of protection.

The product label will state the type of PPE and any specific engineering controls which you must use when handling or applying the pesticide.

If you are using a pesticide under the terms of a specific off-label approval (SOLA), you must follow the guidance on PPE and engineering controls given on the notice of approval.

Similarly, if you are using a commodity substance (see the definition in **annex C**) as a pesticide under the terms of a 'commodity substance approval', you must follow the guidance on PPE and engineering controls given on the notice of approval.

In some situations, a COSHH assessment may show that any PPE or engineering controls stated on the product label or on the relevant notice of approval need to be increased. This may be necessary if you intend to do any of the following:

↘ Apply the pesticide in a mixture with another pesticide or an adjuvant (a substance that is not a pesticide but that increases the effect of the pesticide);

↘ Use the pesticide in a confined space or other difficult situation it is not normally used in;

↘ Work with a pesticide for more than eight hours during any day;

↘ Apply the pesticide as a reduced-volume spray (applying a pesticide in a lower volume of water than the minimum volume recommended on the label for that dose);

↘ Apply the pesticide in a way not recommended on the label or on the relevant notices of approval. (For example, if you are using hand-held equipment in situations where vehicle-mounted or equipment on a trailer would normally be used.); and

↘ Perform tasks not mentioned on the label or on the relevant notice of approval. (For example, when you are entering a newly treated area or checking, repairing or cleaning contaminated equipment.)

When your COSHH assessment shows that the PPE specified on the product label or the relevant notices of approval needs to be increased, you should refer to the general guidance on appropriate PPE in **annex E**.

In all situations, even when the product label or relevant notice of approval does not refer to PPE, it is good practice to wear basic PPE (such as coveralls, suitable protective gloves and boots) at all times when handling and applying pesticides.

You should also consider using PPE if you are a professional gardener who uses products for hobby gardening (amateur pesticides from local shops, garden centres, DIY stores and so on). This is especially the case if you are using a product in large quantities, more often or for a longer period of time than would be the case for a typical hobby gardener.

*The HSE publishes practical advice and guidance on choosing, using and maintaining respiratory protective equipment (RPE) (covered in the HSE booklet HSG53) and other types of personal protective equipment (PPE).*

**ANY PPE MUST BE SUITABLE FOR THE PURPOSE, INCLUDING BEING CORRECTLY MATCHED TO THE JOB AND TO YOU.**

### 3.5.6 SUITABLE PERSONAL PROTECTION EQUIPMENT

Your PPE must keep to any relevant conditions of approval for the pesticide (as shown on the product label and any notice of approval). All PPE must be made to an appropriate standard. Equipment that meets European standards will carry the CE mark. You should make sure that your PPE (including RPE) is CE marked. Look out for this when you use new PPE.

Remember that general workwear (cotton, poly-cotton or nylon overalls or two-piece suits) is not likely to meet the appropriate standards for protective clothing when working with pesticides. Also, when you choose and use a disposable mask over your nose and mouth, you should remember that:

↘ 'nuisance dust masks', which are commonly used by farmers and crofters when carrying out dusty tasks, are not suitable when using pesticides; and

↘ you should dispose of the mask (safely and legally) at the end of each working day, or more often if it is significantly contaminated.

Any PPE must be suitable for the purpose, including being correctly matched to the job and to you. Your employer (if you have one), should consult you or your safety representative about choosing PPE to make sure it fits and is suitable for you. Your employer should pay particular attention to the following:

↘ The nature of the pesticide and the level of exposure;

↘ The PPE's protection, taking account of:

- the environment the equipment will be worn in (for example, snag-free clothing will be needed because of the environment);

- the nature of the work being carried out;

- how long the equipment has to be worn for;

- whether it is compatible with other clothing conditions such as high-visibility clothing and protective head gear; and

- comfort and fit when working in hot and humid conditions.

↘ Whether the pesticide can pass through the material the equipment is made of.

↘ Any limits on the PPE's performance, as stated in any relevant approved standard or by the manufacturer.

↘ The face-fit (seal) of respiratory protective equipment (RPE) which has to be close-fitting (most types other than air-fed visors and helmets).

# WORKING PROCEDURES TO PREVENT OR CONTROL EXPOSURE MUST BE REVIEWED TO MAKE SURE THEY ARE STILL EFFECTIVE.

*You can get information on testing the face-fit of RPE from the HSE website (www.hse.gov.uk).*

The PPE you use will only be effective if you wear it correctly all the time you need it. In some situations, using PPE carelessly or using unsuitable PPE may result in a higher, rather than a lower, risk of operator contamination.

### 3.5.7 MAINTAINING CONTROL MEASURES

Engineering controls and PPE will only be effective and meet the COSHH regulations if they are maintained properly.

Keeping control measures in good repair usually means:

- carrying out regular checks and more detailed inspections;

- checking any equipment that detects faults; and

- carrying out preventive servicing and repair work to put right any fault that could reduce the level of protection. Any faults reported must be put right quickly. Never use equipment that is faulty.

Your employer should make sure that engineering control measures, such as closed-transfer systems or specialised pesticide dispensing systems are:

- checked at the beginning of the treatment season and before each use; and

- examined in detail and tested at suitable intervals.

Working procedures to prevent or control exposure must be reviewed to make sure they are still effective.

You should check your PPE (including RPE), before, during and after each day's use and report any problems to your employer (if you have one). Damaged items must be replaced before you carry out further work with pesticides.

*The BCPC booklet 'Safety Equipment Handbook' gives guidance on how to choose, use and maintain PPE and RPE (see annex B).*

You and your employer (if you have one) must also make sure that RPE is thoroughly examined for signs of deterioration and, where appropriate, tested at least once a month. This testing should be carried out more often if conditions are particularly severe. You or your employer must keep records of these examinations and tests, and correct any faults before the RPE is used.

It is important to:

- remove any contaminated PPE as soon as possible to avoid an increased risk of exposure;

- thoroughly wash your protective gloves inside and out at the end of each day's use, taking care not to contaminate yourself or the environment, especially water;

- dispose of your protective gloves safely and legally after use if the product label tells you to do this or if the gloves are not in a good condition;

- dispose of other contaminated PPE safely and legally or, where appropriate, clean it in line with the manufacturer's instructions and in a way which is safe for people and the environment;

- take appropriate precautions if you need to handle contaminated PPE or other contaminated items; and

- make sure that contaminated protective clothing is never washed with domestic or personal items.

PPE should be kept in suitable storage facilities to keep it clean, dry, well ventilated and secure. Separate storage will be needed for personal clothing, such as coats and other items you remove while you are working with pesticides.

PREPARATION

# YOU MUST PROVIDE PERMANENT, CONVENIENT AND ACCESSIBLE WASHING FACILITIES, IN A PLACE WHERE THEY DO NOT BECOME CONTAMINATED.

### 3.5.8 WELFARE FACILITIES

If you have any staff, (full or part time, casual or permanent) you must provide permanent, convenient and accessible washing facilities, in a place where they do not become contaminated. These facilities will be extra to the washing and decontamination equipment carried on the application equipment or available where the pesticide is being used.

### 3.5.9 WHAT YOU NEED TO DO

You must:

- work in a safe way and use all the appropriate engineering control measures available;

- wear suitable PPE and make sure it fits properly;

- report any problems with engineering controls or your PPE and not use damaged or faulty protective equipment;

- remove contaminated PPE, wash affected skin and put on clean PPE before continuing to work;

- keep PPE in the storage provided when you are not using it and after carrying out appropriate cleaning and maintenance;

- before eating, drinking, smoking or using the toilet, take off any PPE which could contaminate food, drink or cigarettes; and

- maintain a high standard of personal hygiene by making full and proper use of the washing facilities provided.

# THE PURPOSE OF MONITORING HEALTH IS TO PROTECT WORKERS' HEALTH BY DETECTING, AT AN EARLY STAGE, ANY HARM WHICH MAY BE CAUSED BY BEING EXPOSED TO DANGEROUS SUBSTANCES.

## 3.6 MONITORING EXPOSURE AND HEALTH SURVEILLANCE

*You can find advice on monitoring methods in HSE Guidance Note HS (G) 173 'Monitoring Strategies for Toxic Substances'*

### 3.6.1 WHEN IS IT NECESSARY TO MONITOR EXPOSURE TO PESTICIDES?

Monitoring exposure can include:

⊾ wearing personal sampling equipment to measure your exposure to a substance, when carrying out your normal work;

⊾ using fixed sampling equipment to measure the levels of a substance in the workplace air; and

⊾ measuring and assessing the level of a substance or its metabolites (substances the body changes the chemical into) in your breath, urine or blood. This biological monitoring may look into the concentration of the pesticide or metabolite, or look for the effects of the exposure.

Employers do not usually need to monitor their employees' exposure to a pesticide if:

⊾ the pesticide is used in line with the conditions of the product approval and the manufacturer's recommendations; and

⊾ the necessary control measures are properly used and maintained.

However, under the COSHH regulations, there are circumstances where employers must make sure that their employees' exposure to dangerous substances is monitored by competent people. These circumstances include:

⊾ when the failure of the control measures could result in a serious health problem, because of the pesticide itself or the length of exposure;

⊾ when measurements need to be taken to make sure a Workplace Exposure Limit (WEL) is not exceeded; or

⊾ when necessary as an extra check on the effectiveness of control measures. For example, to check the level of contamination affecting respiratory protective equipment.

If the substance being used has been given an exposure limit, testing samples of the workplace atmosphere, usually in the worker's breathing zone, will find out whether the necessary standards are being met.

*You can find information on those chemicals which have a WEL in the latest version of the HSE publication EH40.*

### 3.6.2 WHAT IS HEALTH SURVEILLANCE?

The purpose of monitoring health (known as health surveillance) is to protect workers' health by detecting, at an early stage, any harm which may be caused by being exposed to dangerous substances. It also helps employers to judge the effectiveness of their control measures and their COSHH assessment. The COSHH assessment should identify the need to check the health of employees who could be exposed to dangerous substances.

Health surveillance covers a wide range of activities including:

⊾ keeping health records;

⊾ trained supervisors checking for signs of disease;

⊾ examinations by qualified nurses or doctors; and

⊾ monitoring sick leave.

Health surveillance (other than medical examinations) can be carried out by suitably trained people who do not need to be medically qualified.

**EMPLOYERS SHOULD CONSULT WORKERS OR THEIR SAFETY REPRESENTATIVES WHEN CONSIDERING POSSIBLE HEALTH PROBLEMS.**

### 3.6.3 WHEN IS HEALTH SURVEILLANCE NECESSARY?

*You can find more advice on health surveillance procedures in the HSE 'Approved code of practice on the COSHH Regulations' (L5) and in the HSE booklet 'Health surveillance at work' (HSG61).*

Under the COSHH regulations, employers must make sure that their employees are placed under suitable health surveillance if:

↘ an identifiable disease or health problem may be related to them being exposed to pesticide;

↘ there is a reasonable chance that the disease or problem may be caused by the particular conditions of work; and

↘ there are valid techniques for detecting the disease or problem.

Employers should consult workers or their safety representatives when considering possible health problems. In practice, the pesticides most likely to cause problems are those that can cause skin disorders or can affect nerve cells. These products, usually organophosphates, will be labelled with the warning:

'This product is an anticholinesterase organophosphorus (or carbamate or similar) compound. Do not use if under medical advice not to work with such compounds.'

*Employers can find advice about biological monitoring for staff working with anticholinesterase products in HSE Guidance Note MS 17 'Biological monitoring of workers exposed to organophosphorus pesticides'.*

If it is reasonably likely that health could be harmed, health surveillance should include biological monitoring (testing the breath, urine and blood) of employees to detect the level of exposure or to look for signs of unwanted effects. This monitoring should be carried out under the supervision of a registered medical practitioner.

Any registered medical practitioner supervising the biological monitoring should be familiar with the risks associated with the substances being investigated and the general principles of health surveillance.

### 3.6.4 WHAT ELSE DO EMPLOYERS NEED TO DO?

Employers may need to reconsider their COSHH assessments in the light of the results of health surveillance.

Under the COSHH regulations, employers must keep a health record for each employee who undergoes health surveillance.

### 3.6.5 WHAT ABOUT SUDDEN ILLNESS?

If you, or people you are working with or near, feel unwell as a result of being exposed to pesticides, think about getting immediate medical attention (depending on the nature and severity of the symptoms).

Employers should make sure that any employee who is taken ill while or after working with pesticides sees a doctor (GP or hospital accident and emergency department), where necessary. Send information on the pesticide involved, labels, safety data sheets and possible causes of contamination with the patient.

Employers should not allow any employee affected by being exposed to a pesticide to continue to work with pesticides until the doctor says that it is safe to do so.

Employers and self-employed people must report these incidents under the Reporting of Injuries, Diseases and Dangerous Occurrences Regulations (RIDDOR) 1995. If you are not sure whether an incident needs to be reported, contact your nearest HSE office to check (the address and phone number will be in The Phone Book under 'Health and Safety Executive'). For emergencies, outside office hours, phone 0151 922 9235.

*You can get a guide to the Reporting of Injuries, Diseases and Dangerous Occurrences Regulations (RIDDOR) 1995 from the HSE. You can get further details from HSE Information Services by phoning 0845 3450055 (see annex D).*

PREPARATION

# YOU SHOULD CONSIDER HOW EXPOSURE MIGHT AFFECT MEMBERS OF THE PUBLIC.

## 3.7 PROTECTING THE PUBLIC

### 3.7.1 NEIGHBOURING PROPERTY

You must make sure that the pesticides you apply are targeted at the land, crop, structure, material or area you want to treat. Pesticide drifting off target can cause problems between pesticide users and their neighbours. It can also harm wildlife and damage gardens. You must remember that pesticides which are dust or fine granules can drift. Make sure you apply them in the appropriate weather conditions and with the correct equipment that is properly adjusted for the product you are using.

You should consider how exposure might affect members of the public. You should also consider whether you are applying pesticides near to homes, schools, nursing homes, hospitals, environmentally sensitive areas, organic farms and so on. It is good management to consider if you need to take any extra measures when applying pesticides near these premises. This may include spraying when people are out at work or when schools are closed, or leaving an untreated area next to the neighbouring property or area. If you need to make a COSHH assessment for the pesticide product you are using, you should include this factor within it.

Telling people before you apply a pesticide gives those people who might be affected information about the pesticide, but this is not an alternative to measures to control exposure. It is good practice for you to give information about the pesticide and the reason for using it to anyone who has concerns about pesticides. People often do not know that there is a positive approvals process and that precautions are taken to keep negative effects outside the target area as low as possible.

If you receive payments under the Single Farm Payment Scheme (and certain other payment support schemes) you must meet cross compliance requirements which have been developed to protect the environment and public, animal and plant health. The Common Agricultural Policy Schemes (Cross Compliance) (Scotland) Regulations 2004 (SSI No 518) make this the law. Even if you are not getting a Single Farm Payment, when you are using pesticides you must make sure you use an approved product and follow the instructions on the label, taking account of recommended best practice. Agri-environment schemes such as the Rural Stewardship Scheme give farmers and crofters opportunities to make the environment on their own farm or croft better, and reward them for it. The Schemes may involve you setting up field margins and carrying out other environmental management to encourage biodiversity, improve water quality and protect the countryside and the historic environment.

*To find more information on cross compliance you should look at the Scottish Executive website: www.scotland.gov.uk/Topics/Agriculture/grants/ Schemes/ccompliance. If you want details of the rural stewardship scheme, go to www. scotland.gov.uk/Topics/Agriculture/Environment/ Agrienvironment/RuralSteward/RSSintro*

### 3.7.2 WHEN MUST NOTICE BE GIVEN?

There may be people, authorities or organisations you need to contact before you can use the pesticide you have chosen. You should always read the label first to find out. For example:

⊾ If you apply pesticides from a helicopter or fixed-wing aircraft, by law you must give the public notice about the spraying (see **annex G**);

⊾ The conditions of approval for certain pesticides may contain detailed conditions for giving people notice and displaying warning notices. You must follow these conditions;

⊾ Before you use any product approved for use in or near water (this is usually a herbicide used to remove plants in or around water) contact the Scottish Environment Protection Agency. You may also have to let water abstractors know;

⊾ You must also contact Scottish Natural Heritage if you intend to use a pesticide in a specially designated area; and

⊾ You might need to tell beekeepers or the local beekeepers' spray liaison officer. This is explained fully in **paragraph 3.8.5**.

*If you are using sulphuric acid as an agricultural desiccant (drying agent), or using another commodity substance for an approved pesticidal use, you must act in line with all the conditions of use set out in the appropriate commodity substance approval. You can get this approval from PSD or look at their website (www. pesticides.gov.uk/approvals.asp?id=311).*

Guidance on using sulphuric acid as an agricultural desiccant in a safe and legal way is given in the 'Code of best practice: safe use of sulphuric acid as an agricultural desiccant' produced by the National Association of Agricultural Contractors (NAAC) (see www.naac.co.uk/Codes/acidcode.asp).

### 3.7.3 GIVING NOTICE TO BYSTANDERS AND OCCUPIERS OF NEIGHBOURING PROPERTY

By law, you do not have to leave an unsprayed buffer zone between a treated area and neighbouring property. When you spray right up to a neighbour's boundary you increase the risk of the pesticide going onto their property. You must not allow spray to drift onto their property as the law states that any person who uses a pesticide must confine the use of that pesticide to the land, crop, structure, material or other area being treated.

PREPARATION

**REMEMBER, GIVING NOTICE TO NEIGHBOURS DOES NOT REMOVE THE NEED FOR YOU TO TAKE MEASURES TO CONTROL EXPOSURE.**

If you apply pesticides as instructed on the label and follow the general advice of this code, they should not pose a significant risk to the health of people outside the area being treated. It is a good idea to think about the following:

↘ Applying pesticides may attract the attention of members of the public. Some products have information cards to give to interested people. It is usually pesticides used in amenity areas (such as parks) which attract most interest from the public, and it is these products which usually have information cards;

↘ It is often best to be considerate to neighbours, such as spraying when people are at work, when the school is closed, and so on;

↘ It is generally good practice to tell the people who occupy land, premises or houses close to the area that you will apply pesticides to;

↘ You may want to think about whether a sign would be the easiest way of telling people about the pesticide used and where they can get further information. (Remember to take the signs down afterwards.);

↘ You should also consider telling neighbours who grow organic or sensitive crops when you are planning to apply a pesticide. If you are a contractor, you may want to check this point with the person to whom you are contracted;

↘ You should take particular care when applying pesticides near hospitals, schools, retirement homes and so on. For instance, children may come to the boundary of their play areas to watch you. In these cases, you should assess if you need to tell the person in charge of the premises that you are going to apply pesticides and, if necessary, agree any extra precautions that you and they should take; and

↘ When you look at any COSHH assessment you have done, or make any other judgement to control risks to people you think are vulnerable, your measures may include leaving an untreated area next to the neighbouring property or changing the time of the application.

Remember, giving notice to neighbours does not remove the need for you to take measures to control exposure.

# THE SCOTTISH OUTDOOR ACCESS CODE PROVIDES DETAILED GUIDANCE ON THE RESPONSIBILITIES OF THOSE EXERCISING ACCESS RIGHTS AND OF THOSE MANAGING LAND AND WATER.

## 3.7.4 PUBLIC ACCESS RIGHTS

When applying pesticides to crops or other areas to be treated, you must take proper care for the interests of people who are exercising or seeking to exercise their access rights. The Land Reform (Scotland) Act 2003 (see annex A) gives everyone statutory access rights to most land and inland water in Scotland. Land in which crops have been sown or are growing is excluded from access rights, but access rights may be exercised on the field margins and in other fields. In some locations an arable field may be crossed by paths including core paths or rights of way.

The Scottish Outdoor Access Code provides detailed guidance on the responsibilities of those exercising access rights and of those managing land and water. The Code states that people exercising access rights should follow any precautions over the use of a particular route or area while particular activities are being carried out, but also states that these precautions need to be reasonable and practicable.

Application of a pesticide on a path may result in a health risk for those using the path, particularly until the spray has dried. Pets could also be affected. You should therefore take special care not to let your pesticide drift onto paths and areas likely to be used by members of the public exercising their access rights. You may need to stop working when people are using paths or adjacent ground.

Before applying a pesticide, you should take all reasonably practical steps to protect people's safety. In particular it is advisable to carry out a risk assessment (a COSHH assessment is a legal requirement for many pesticides, see section 3.4) and you should follow the pesticide's instructions.

Where a risk cannot be prevented or adequately controlled by other means, then the precautions could include providing advice to help in managing access within the affected area. Relevant information should be provided, explaining the nature, location and duration of the risk. Suitable alternative routes may be provided in some cases. You might use notices to ask people not to use a particular route or area for a specific time period, or not to do a particular activity whilst there is still a danger. For example, it might be safe for someone to walk through a field, but not to picnic, for a set period after the operation. Templates for such notices are available (see further information at 3.7.6).

Generally, the higher the likely levels of public access (such as along well-used routes, at popular places or at the weekend) or the more dangerous an operation is likely to be, the more you need to give information or identify alternative routes. The action you take needs to be appropriate for the level of risk as it is assessed, which depends on the nature of the work, the site and the levels of public access expected.

PREPARATION

Occasionally you may use a product which could present a specific risk for those coming into contact with it (for instance, a product that sets a period of time before anyone can re-enter the area). In such circumstances you should keep the following in mind:

- You should take all possible steps to make sure that, when you are treating other areas with a pesticide, paths and public access areas do not get accidentally sprayed with the product or have any drift fall onto them;

- If a path crosses or runs alongside a field or other area to be treated, members of the public should not be exposed to drift as you apply the pesticides. You may want to consider using notices to warn people that pesticides are being applied and telling people to keep themselves, children and pets on the path;

- If members of the public are using the path, you must temporarily stop applying the pesticide if there is a risk of them being exposed. You should also know about any paths or access rights in areas next to that being treated so you can stop if you need to;

- Except for when you are using sulphuric acid, you should use advisory notices, and not put up notices or any other restriction to physically stop people from exercising their access rights;

- You will need to take special care in areas of open country and other amenity or forestry areas the public have access to. In these situations (for example, when you are spraying bracken), you should display suitable warning notices at the main access points. These access points may be where the public leave the tarred road or car park and should be a considerable distance from the application site. In the notices you may want to suggest an alternative route;

- Always remember to take warning notices down when they are no longer needed. Take account of any remaining risks, such as to children and pets straying into freshly treated areas. With some pesticides, unprotected people and livestock should be kept out of the treated area for a specific period. Do not use these pesticides if you cannot restrict access to the site for the necessary period; and

- You should follow the guidance given in this section about the safety of people and animals, as appropriate, when you treat paths to control weeds in amenity areas. You should also consider how safe and legal the intended use is when applying a pesticide with equipment mounted on or pulled by a vehicle on paths. You should consult and, if necessary, get the permission of, the local authority or owner of the path before you carry out this work.

### 3.7.5 WHO SHOULD I TELL IF THERE IS AN INCIDENT INVOLVING PESTICIDES?

You should report any incident involving people and pesticides to your nearest HSE office (the address and phone number will be in The Phone Book under 'Health and Safety Executive'). The HSE Information Line number is 0845 345 0055 (they should be able to tell you the number of the local office). For emergencies outside office hours you should ring 0151 922 9235. You can get further details from HSE Information Services (see **annex D**).

Certain incidents need to be reported under the Reporting of Injuries, Diseases and Dangerous Occurrences Regulations (RIDDOR) 1995. You can get a guide to these regulations from HSE. If you are not sure whether an incident needs to be reported, phone the HSE to check.

You can find out the role of the Pesticide Incident Appraisal Panel at www.hse.gov.uk or from the address given in **annex D**.

# THE INFORMATION ON THE PRODUCT LABEL WILL PROVIDE THE BASIS FOR YOUR ENVIRONMENTAL RISK ASSESSMENT.

PREPARATION

### 3.7.6 FURTHER INFORMATION

More information on paths and access rights in Scotland is available from the website www.outdooraccess-scotland.com. This website includes a range of information for land managers, including guidance on the use of signs, (www.outdooraccess-scotland.com/upload/Signs%20guidance%20for%20l and%20managers2.pdf) and it also provides templates for signs to be used in advising people of land management operations like spraying pesticides, (www.outdooraccess-scotland.com/upload/Land%20Management%20460x1 30mm.pdf).

You can also get information including the Scottish Outdoor Access Code from Scottish Natural Heritage at www.snh.org.uk or by contacting them at the address in **annex D**.

## 3.8 PROTECTING WILDLIFE AND THE ENVIRONMENT

*The Pesticides Forum booklet 'Pesticide use – the environmental issues' provides background information on the major environmental issues associated with using pesticides. See the PSD website (www. pesticides.gov.uk).*

### 3.8.1 ASSESSING POSSIBLE NEGATIVE EFFECTS

When you are planning to use a pesticide you should assess the impact on biodiversity. The Scottish Biodiversity Strategy produced by the Scottish Executive, in conjunction with the Scottish Biodiversity Forum, provides a framework for the protection and enhancement of Scotland's biodiversity (see www.biodiversityscotland.gov.uk). Guidance at a UK level is also available from the UK Biodiversity Partnership (see www.ukbap.org.uk).

The information on the product label will provide the basis for your environmental risk assessment.

Further information, in the form of an environmental information sheet (EIS), is available for some products.

*You can download all available environmental information sheets from the Voluntary Initiative website (www.voluntaryinitiative.org.uk).*

Drawing up a plan to protect crops, such as a LEAF audit (a way of reviewing and improving your farming practices, perhaps to help you take up integrated farm management, improve efficiency and reduce costs) or crop protection management plan (CPMP) will help you to make sure that you are taking a planned approach to reducing the environmental effect of using pesticides on your farm or holding. Details are available on the Voluntary Initiative website (www.voluntaryinitiative.org.uk).

## REMEMBER THE IMPORTANCE OF HABITATS FOR WILDLIFE AND WILD PLANTS WHEN PLANNING TO USE PESTICIDES, ESPECIALLY WHERE THERE ARE SENSITIVE AREAS.

### 3.8.2 HOW CAN WILDLIFE AND PLANTS BE PROTECTED?

Remember the importance of habitats for wildlife and wild plants when planning to use pesticides, especially where there are sensitive areas such as:

↘ hedges;

↘ ditches, ponds and so on;

↘ wetlands and water margins;

↘ rough grazing and grassland rich in different plants and creatures; and

↘ scrub woodlands.

These areas are usually relatively insignificant as sources of pests or diseases. You should avoid contaminating them with pesticides, either directly or from drift, to protect beneficial or harmless insects and other wildlife. Similarly, contamination by herbicides could kill a wide range of wild plants and may encourage aggressive weed species to become established. It is important that you recognise these sensitive features in the area to be treated, assess the risks to them and protect them appropriately, possibly by keeping untreated buffer zones.

By law, you must not kill or damage any wild animal or plant species specified under the Wildlife and Countryside Act 1981 or appearing on the list of European protected species (like bats). You may need to get a licence from the Scottish Executive if you need to apply a pesticide in a situation which might affect any of these species. Further information is available on the Scottish Executive website (www.scotland.gov.uk/Topics/Environment/Wildlife-Habitats).

If you are not familiar with the layout of the area you intend to treat, or the location of sensitive features, conservation headlands and buffer zones (this might be the case if you are a contractor), you could accidentally damage these areas. In this situation, it is important that the owner or occupier of the land briefs you fully before you use a pesticide.

Under the terms of the Common Agricultural Policy (CAP), cross compliance provides protection for boundary features including hedgerows, trees and watercourses. To minimise the potential for damage it is recommended that activities such as pesticide spraying is not carried out within two metres of field margins, the banks of watercourses or the base of hedges. However, you may need to leave a larger buffer zone when you are using certain pesticides (this will be shown on the product label) to protect plants and creatures you are not treating, including fish and water.

# YOU SHOULD TAKE SPECIAL CARE WHEN USING PESTICIDES ON, OR NEAR, ANY LAND COVERED BY AN AGRI-ENVIRONMENT AGREEMENT.

For field crops, you may be able to set up a permanent grass margin to prevent weeds moving into the crop, while providing a habitat for wildlife (including beneficial insects) and protecting hedgerows and watercourses.

In some situations, you may be able to set up a 'conservation headland' usually the outermost six metres, to allow grasses and broad-leaved plants to grow and to encourage the insects that live on them. These insects are food for farmland wildlife and birds. Where there are conservation headlands, you should follow agreed management principles to avoid any risk to other plants and animals. The labels of some pesticides will have specific restrictions which you must keep to.

You should take special care when using pesticides on, or near, any land covered by an agri-environment agreement.

***You can get more information on protecting field margins and conservation headlands from The Game Conservancy Trust, the Farm and Wildlife Advisory Group (FWAG), Linking Environment and Farming (LEAF) and the Royal Society for the Protection of Birds (RSPB).***

### 3.8.3 SPECIALLY DESIGNATED AREAS
Some areas have a special status in law, for example:

- local nature reserves (LNR);
- national nature reserves (NNR);
- sites of special scientific interest (SSSI);
- special areas of conservation (SAC); and
- special protection areas (SPA).

Some of these areas (SPAs and SACs) are recognised as important European habitats ('Natura 2000 sites') and some are recognised as wetlands of international importance ('Ramsar sites'). All these sites must be protected from any possible harmful effects resulting from using pesticides in or near them.

If you are uncertain about the measures you should take to protect SSSIs, SACs, SPAs and Ramsar sites, consult Scottish Natural Heritage (SNH) before you apply pesticides. In some situations, it may be illegal to use pesticides without permission from SNH. If you intend to apply pesticides from an aircraft near these areas, you must follow specific rules (see annex G).

Normally, the owner or occupier of the area to be treated is responsible for giving notice to Scottish Natural Heritage and getting any permission needed before pesticides are applied. However, if the treatment will be carried out by a person or company applying pesticides as a commercial service, the person applying the pesticide should:

- discuss with the owner or occupier of the area to be treated whether the area or its surroundings need special consideration; and

- ask if the necessary notice has been given and any necessary permission received.

Detailed treatment records are particularly important if pesticide is being used on, or near, these sites.

### 3.8.4 HOW CAN WILD BIRDS AND MAMMALS BE PROTECTED?
Wild birds and mammals, including pets, are at particular risk from treated seed and from pesticides in granule, pellet or bait form. Make sure you follow all precautions and advice on product labels to protect birds and mammals. In some situations you will need to take special care, such as if water voles are at risk of poisoning from vertebrate control agents.

You must make sure that all treated seed is properly covered by soil, and that soil-incorporated granules and pellets are not left on the soil surface. Also, you must not leave any spilt granules, pellets or treated seeds lying around. When you are test-baiting using pesticides, make sure that you protect the baits to prevent poisoning of species you are not targeting.

### 3.8.5 HOW CAN BEES BE PROTECTED?

***Contact details for the Scottish Beekeepers' Association Spray Co-ordinator can be found on the Association's website at www. scottishbeekeepers.org.uk***

Products that may harm bees will be labelled as 'harmful', 'dangerous', 'extremely dangerous' or 'high risk' to bees. You should tell the beekeepers identified in your environmental risk assessment, or the beekeepers' spray liaison officer, 48 hours before you plan to use a pesticide at the times of the year when bees are at risk or whenever you intend to use a pesticide that specifically harms bees. This will allow beekeepers to take the necessary precautions. You should also tell beekeepers if you change your plans.

After you choose the most appropriate pesticide you should also consider the measures for protecting bees set out in **table 3** below.

**TABLE 3** Measures for protecting bees

| Do | Do not |
|---|---|
| ↘ check for bees visiting plants and remember that the honeydew produced by aphids is attractive to bees | ↘ spray unless you have to |
| ↘ follow closely the environmental protection instructions on the label and the guidance in this code | ↘ use pesticides labelled 'harmful', 'dangerous', 'extremely dangerous' or 'high risk' to bees if crops or weeds are in open flower or part bloom, unless this is allowed by the product label |
| ↘ spray in the evening when bees have stopped flying, as this allows several hours for the pesticide to dry before bees become active again, (but remember that bumblebees might be around to look for food later into the evening than honeybees) | ↘ let pesticide drift into bee hives or into hedgerows or fields where bees, including bumblebees, may be looking for food |
| ↘ choose a cool cloudy day, or the early morning (if you have to spray during the day) | |

### 3.8.6 OTHER BENEFICIAL SPECIES

Your assessment of the environmental risks needs to take account of the effect pesticides have on other beneficial insects (like ladybirds and lacewings) and other species in general. The product label may state that you must not apply pesticide to a margin around the treated area. Also, the product label may specify or recommend other spraying restrictions to protect these species (such as spraying before a certain date).

### 3.8.7 LIVESTOCK

Any period of time when animals need to be kept away from the treated area will be specified on the product label. Make sure you follow this instruction.

Some poisonous weeds, such as ragwort, can become more attractive to grazing animals after they have been treated with herbicides. It is good practice to keep livestock (including horses) out of treated areas until the weeds have died and completely disappeared whether or not the product label of the herbicide used says that livestock have to be kept off the land for a set period.

### 3.8.8 FISH AND OTHER AQUATIC LIFE

Fish and other aquatic life (plants and creatures living in water) can be at risk from being exposed to pesticides.

You must leave an untreated buffer zone between the treated area and the top of the bank of a neighbouring watercourse or dry ditch to reduce the amount of pesticide reaching the watercourse.

In some circumstances, you can reduce the size of a buffer zone to protect aquatic life if a local environment risk assessment for pesticides (LERAP) justifies this. The continuing approval of some products may depend on you fully keeping to the LERAP schemes.

Some situations in amenity and forestry situations do not come under the scope of the LERAP schemes.

The product label will state whether a pesticide needs a buffer zone to protect aquatic life and whether this buffer zone may be reduced after a LERAP.

*You can find detailed guidance on how to carry out and record a LERAP when applying pesticides in the Scottish Executive booklet 'Local environment risk assessment for pesticides: horizontal boom sprayers' which can be downloaded from the Scottish Executive website at www.scotland.gov. uk/library3/environment/hbsl-00.asp and the Defra booklet 'Local environment risk assessment for pesticides: broadcast air-assisted sprayers', available from the PSD website at www.pesticides.gov.uk/fg_leraps.asp?id=207.*

When you use accredited low-drift spraying equipment (both nozzles and complete spraying systems) under the LERAP schemes, you must use the equipment exactly as explained on the PSD website.

By law you must record the reasons for LERAP decisions, even if you have chosen not to reduce the buffer zone shown on the product label to reflect local conditions.

You must keep all records for three years from the date you use the product.

The LERAP schemes for protecting watercourses and dry ditches do not apply to kerbside gullies, French drains, swales or similar structures often present in amenity and industrial areas. In these situations, you should take all the necessary precautions to avoid contaminating surface water and groundwater and you should follow the guidance for applying pesticides on hard surfaces.

Similarly, the LERAP schemes do not apply in situations where temporary ditches which do not run into watercourses are created, such as in some forestry operations.

PREPARATION

# MOST POISONING CAUSED BY PESTICIDES IS THE RESULT OF THE PRODUCT BEING MISUSED OR DELIBERATELY ABUSED WITH THE INTENTION OF KILLING AN ANIMAL OR A BIRD.

**3.8.9** WILDLIFE INCIDENT INVESTIGATION SCHEME (WIIS)

Incidents involving pesticides are put into one of three groups:

↘ Approved use: where the product has been used in line with the law;

↘ Abuse: deliberately trying to poison animals with pesticides not approved for that purpose; and

↘ Misuse: carelessly or accidentally not following correct practice.

Very occasionally, using an approved pesticide correctly may result in animals, birds or other wildlife being accidentally poisoned. However, most poisoning caused by pesticides is the result of the product being misused or deliberately abused with the intention of killing an animal or a bird. This happens in town areas as well as the countryside. This poisoning is against the law and may result in you being prosecuted.

If you find wild animals, birds, livestock, domestic animals, honeybees or beneficial insects which you suspect have been affected by pesticides, or if you find spilt pesticide or baits, phone the WIIS on 0800 321 600. For incidents involving fish, phone the Scottish Environment Protection Agency on 0800 807060. If appropriate, an officer will investigate the situation to see if it is caused by a pesticide or some other chemical. Appropriate action can then be taken.

Avoid contact with dead animal carcasses, spilt baits, pesticides or containers and never try to unblock a badger sett or fox earth which may have been gassed.

### 3.8.10 PREVENTING PESTICIDES FROM CONTAMINATING SURFACE WATER AND GROUNDWATER

Very small amounts of a pesticide concentrate can have a significant effect on water. A spillage of only 1 gram of active ingredient - which could be the residue on a single foil seal from a container - will need to be diluted by 10 million litres of water to meet the European maximum limit for a pesticide in drinking water. This is the amount of water needed to fill a stream 1 metre wide and 0.3 metres deep for 35 kilometres (22 miles).

Water can be contaminated, either directly or indirectly, with pesticides. This could have serious consequences for the environment. A small number of pesticides are specifically approved for being used in or near water, and only those products must be used.

When applying pesticide near watercourses you should:

↘ take appropriate precautions to reduce spray drift;

↘ follow any buffer zone and LERAP conditions for protecting fish and other aquatic life; and

↘ where appropriate (such as when using a pesticide in or directly on the banks of a watercourse), spray upstream.

Watercourses can also be contaminated by pesticides reaching field drainage systems through the soil. You should take care to avoid applying pesticides when the risk of them getting into drainage systems is high. Schemes to reduce this problem have been agreed with pesticide manufacturers and users of specific pesticides.

***You can get more information on the Crop Protection Association website (www.cropprotection.org.uk) and on the Voluntary Initiative website (www.voluntaryinitiative.org.uk).***

Groundwater (the law describes this as 'all water which is below the surface of the ground and in direct contact with the ground or soil') can be contaminated by pesticides. There are some circumstances when using an approved pesticide correctly may present a risk to groundwater. For example, if a water table is near the surface, or there is thin soil, very sandy soil or cracked limestone bedrock, pesticides may move rapidly through the ground and enter groundwater.

PREPARATION

# WHATEVER TYPE OF PESTICIDE YOU ARE USING, WHETHER IT IS A SPRAY, GRANULE, PELLET, DUST OR ANY OTHER FORM, YOU SHOULD CARRY OUT ALL MIXING, FILLING OR LOADING OPERATIONS WELL AWAY FROM WATERCOURSES, DITCHES AND DRAINS.

This type of contamination may be of particular concern when the groundwater is feeding a drinking water supply.

↘ In general, you should not use long-lasting pesticides and pesticides that can spread within 50 metres of a spring, well or borehole.

↘ You should carefully consider using any pesticide, especially on quick-draining surfaces such as gravel, hardstandings and similar areas.

↘ You should also take special care to protect groundwater when using pesticides in areas further away from springs, wells and boreholes but still within their 'catchment areas'.

↘ If there is a public water supply nearby, you may need to restrict your pesticide use over a larger area.

*For further advice you should contact your local Scottish Environment Protection Agency office.*

Take particular care to protect surface water and groundwater when you:

↘ are preparing a pesticide;

↘ are transporting a pesticide to the area being treated; and

↘ clean equipment and dispose of pesticide waste and containers.

Whatever type of pesticide you are using, whether it is a spray, granule, pellet, dust or any other form, you should carry out all mixing, filling or loading operations well away from watercourses, ditches and drains.

↘ On farms and holdings you should have a specific area for filling sprayers. However, when applying pesticides in other forms (such as granules or pellets), you usually need to load the application equipment in the relevant field.

↘ Similarly, in many amenity and forestry areas, where work is carried out at several separate locations, you will need to mix and load pesticides where they are being applied.

When you can use a dedicated mixing and loading area, this should be designed to prevent pollution of surface water and groundwater. It should:

↘ be where it will not be affected by flooding or by cross-contamination (such as from vehicle movements);

↘ have an impermeable surface (one that does not let liquid pass through it), ideally under cover, which spills can be cleaned up from; and either:

- allow all drainage and run-off to be collected and disposed of using a lined biobed (see **glossary 1** in **annex C**), as described in **table 4** overleaf;

- allow all drainage and run-off to be collected and disposed of using an area of soil or grass or an unlined biobed, as described in **table 4** overleaf; or

- allow all drainage and run-off to be collected and disposed of using a licensed waste-disposal contractor.

TABLE 4 Options for dealing with drainage and run-off from dedicated mixing and loading areas

| You can: | If you: |
| --- | --- |
| dispose of the drainage and run-off from your mixing and loading area to a lined biobed (either directly using a drive-over biobed or using an indirect biobed fed by the drainage from a hard surface) | or the operator of the lined biobed) are appropriately authorised under the Waste Management Licensing Regulations (see **annex A**); and<br><br>collect the water outflow from the base of the lined biobed and reuse it as irrigation water or for preparing spray solutions. |
| dispose of the drainage and run-off from your mixing and loading area on to soil, grass or an unlined biobed (agricultural pesticides only) | are authorised by the Scottish Environment Protection Agency under the Water Environment (Controlled Activities) (Scotland) Regulations 2005 (see **annex A**). |
| collect the drainage and run off from your mixing and loading area | dispose of it through a licensed waste disposal contractor. |

If you need to mix and load the pesticide at the area being treated, you will need to make sure that the site you have chosen is suitable and know about any risks associated with handling pesticides on uneven surfaces.

In all situations you should take care to prevent spills when filling equipment by:

⬐ making sure your equipment is well maintained and does not leak or drip; and

⬐ following the detailed guidance on filling given in the table 5 in section 4.5.

If you spill any pesticide or spray solution, make sure you contain the spillage to keep any contamination as low as possible.

⬐ Do not allow pesticides to get into any yard or field drain, ditch or other watercourse.

⬐ Never hose down a spill.

⬐ Use an inert absorbent material (that is, one that does not react chemically, such as cat litter or dry sand) to soak it up. Dispose of the material safely and legally.

Portable drip trays of various types and sizes are available. They are designed to catch spilt pesticides during mixing and loading operations and to allow any spills to be returned to the equipment. Using a drip tray will help you to prevent contamination of your dedicated filling area or, if you need to fill your equipment at the area to be treated, prevent environmental contamination.

***You can get more guidance on preventing water pollution from the Scottish Executive booklet 'Keeping pesticides out of water', available from the Scottish Executive website at www.scotland.gov. uk/library5/environment/kpow-00.asp.***

When you are driving or transporting equipment to and from the area you are treating, make sure it is not overfilled and cannot leak or drip. Do not go through fords at any time and, if you have an alternative route, it is the best option to avoid crossing watercourses at all, including going over bridges.

To protect groundwater, you must not dispose of pesticide waste onto land in Scotland without an authorisation issued by the Scottish Environment Protection Agency. However, when you use a pesticide in line with the product approval, you do not need a groundwater authorisation.

Whenever possible, you should decontaminate equipment, inside and out, within the area you have treated and avoid using a single dedicated cleaning area. However, you must make sure that, when you apply your washings or unused pesticide within the treated area, you do not go over the maximum application rate for the pesticide product. Generally, repeated flushing of spraying equipment with low volumes of water will be as effective as a single rinse using a large volume of water, and will create less rinse water. If spraying equipment is fitted with a low-volume-tank washing device, use this as recommended by the manufacturer.

You can also wash down sprayers and dispose of surplus spray solution using a lined biobed.

*You can get the latest advice on biobeds from the Scottish Environment Protection Agency.*

In some circumstances you can wash sprayers or dispose of surplus spray solution on areas of soil or grass, or drain hard surfaces used for these purposes to areas of soil or grass under the terms of a licence, known as a CAR licence, issued under The Water Environment (Controlled Activities) (Scotland) Regulations 2005 (see **annex A**) by the Scottish Environment Protection Agency.

You should always store sprayers and other cleaned equipment under cover to avoid contaminated rainwater run-off, which may contaminate groundwater and surface water. For the same reasons, you should store empty pesticide containers, rinsed where appropriate, under cover in a secure area.

When re-stocking forests and woodland or carrying out similar activities involving treated propagating material, keep pesticide-treated plants away from ditches and other surface water. Managers should make sure that planters know about this and do not try to 'freshen up' treated material in this way.

### 3.8.11 CONTROLLING WEEDS IN OR NEAR WATER

*You can get more guidance on using pesticides in or near water in the Defra booklet 'Guidelines for the use of herbicides on weeds in or near watercourses and lakes' and in the Environment Agency book 'Use of herbicides in or near water' and associated guidance notes.*

There may be times when you need to use a pesticide to control weeds in or near water. Aquatic and bank-side plants are an important part of the ecosystem, so you should consider other methods of control before deciding to use a pesticide. If you decide that you need to use a pesticide in or near any water, not just rivers and streams, you must only use one approved specifically for use in or near water. This will be shown on the product label.

3

# YOU SHOULD ALWAYS STORE SPRAYERS AND OTHER CLEANED EQUIPMENT UNDER COVER TO AVOID CONTAMINATED RAINWATER RUN-OFF.

# WHEN YOU ARE PLANNING TO CONTROL ESTABLISHED INVASIVE WEEDS, ALSO CONSIDER THE NEED TO PREVENT FURTHER PROBLEMS (SUCH AS SOIL BEING WORN AWAY) WHICH MAY RESULT AFTER THE WEEDS HAVE BEEN CONTROLLED.

Before you use any product approved for use in or near water you should contact the Scottish Environment Protection Agency. You may also have to let water abstractors know.

As a general principle, when spraying on or near a watercourse with a significant flow you should spray in the opposite direction to the main water flow (that is, always spray 'upstream'). This will reduce the maximum concentration of pesticide that could be present at any one point in the watercourse and so reduces the risk to aquatic life.

### 3.8.12 APPLYING PESTICIDES FROM AN AIRCRAFT

Only certain pesticides are approved for being applied from the air. The specific legal obligations you must meet before, during and after applying a pesticide from the air, as well as details of the consultation process needed to keep the risk to the environment as low as possible, are set out in **annex G**.

### 3.8.13 INVASIVE WEEDS

*You should consult the Scottish Environment Protection Agency to make sure that you are using appropriate control methods. Organisations such as the Cornwall Knotweed Forum, see their website at www.ex.ac.uk/knotweed and the Centre for Aquatic Plant Management (CAPM), www.ceh.ac.uk/sections/wq/CAPM1.htm also provide useful information.*

Invasive and non-native weeds (that is, weeds not natural to the area), which can quickly take over native species, can cause major problems. It is an offence, under Section 14(2) of the Wildlife and Countryside Act 1981 to plant or cause certain non-native plants to grow in the wild. Some plants such as Japanese Knotweed (*Fallopia japonica*) and *Crassula helmsii* (commonly known as New Zealand Pigmy weed or Australian Swamp Stonecrop) are able to re-generate from very small pieces of vegetative material. It is important therefore to find out about the best control methods before taking action and any national programmes which are in place to tackle the problem.

When you are planning to control established invasive weeds, also consider the need to prevent further problems (such as soil being worn away) which may result after the weeds have been controlled. You can get general guidance on the issues associated with controlling invasive weeds from organisations such as Scottish Natural Heritage or the Scottish Environment Protection Agency. For further information, refer to the Horticultural Code of Practice for Scotland – helping to prevent the spread of invasive non-native species (www.scotland.gov.uk/invasivespecies).

# WORKING WITH PESTICIDES

## 4.1 INTRODUCTION TO GUIDANCE

This part of the Code provides guidance on:

↘ how to handle, transport and prepare pesticides for use;

↘ how to use them safely; and

↘ what action to take after using them.

## 4.2 PREPARING TO APPLY PESTICIDES

### 4.2.1 CHECKS TO CARRY OUT

It is important to carry out a series of checks before using any pesticide and regularly during the treatment season, as appropriate. Make sure that you have taken the following action:

✓ Had suitable training and, if necessary, gained a certificate of competence to apply the pesticide in the proposed way.

✓ Read and understood the product label and any extra information relating to off-label uses.

✓ Made a suitable and sufficient COSHH assessment, recorded it and checked that it is still valid.

✓ Put in place any measures to control exposure, and keep these measures up to date. Suitable PPE is available.

✓ Carried out an appropriate environmental risk assessment and made sure that you can keep to any measures to protect wildlife and the environment, such as any buffer zones or other restrictions on use, to protect:

↘ aquatic life (including any LERAP conditions);

↘ bees and other insects and creatures; and

↘ surface water and groundwater.

✓ Taken account of the need to avoid contaminating feed stores or areas that livestock have access to.

✓ Taken measures to meet any conditions on the label for keeping livestock or people out of treated areas for a certain period.

✓ Got advice and, when necessary, received permission from the appropriate agencies, before using pesticides in areas of special environmental status in or near water, from aircraft and, where necessary, on public paths.

✓ ↘ Given adequate notice to occupiers of neighbouring properties and members of the public.

↘ Displayed warning notices.

↘ Followed the specific responsibilities for giving notice when spraying from the air and when spraying sulphuric acid.

↘ Given adequate notice to beekeepers.

✓ Checked equipment for applying pesticide to make sure it is in good working order and is working correctly and accurately.

✓ Put emergency procedures in place and made sure operators have:

  ↘ appropriate emergency equipment such as spill kit and decontamination equipment for skin and eyes;

  ↘ emergency details for the products being used; and

  ↘ a list of emergency contact details for the Scottish Environment Protection Agency and medical services.

✓ Made sure the pesticide can be transported safely and legally to the area you are treating.

✓ Got enough of the correct pesticide to complete the job, and checked the calculations of the amount of pesticide needed for each tank, load or run, possibly allowing for an untreated or under-dosed area for disposing of sprayer washings.

✓ Made appropriate arrangements for cleaning equipment and disposing of any waste pesticide and pesticide packaging (such as containers, closures and foil seals) safely and legally.

## 4.2.2 DANGEROUS PRACTICES

The following activities are dangerous when pesticides are being used. They should be forbidden by employers and never practised by anyone using pesticides.

↘ Sucking or blowing (by mouth) any nozzle, pipe connection or device which forms part of the equipment for applying pesticide.

↘ Continuing to work after being contaminated. (You should immediately remove all contaminated items of clothing, wash the affected skin and put on clean clothing before starting again.)

You should also make sure that you do not eat, drink, smoke or go to the toilet while working with pesticides. You should carry out these activities outside the treated area, after you have removed your PPE and washed your hands and face.

Read the product label before opening any pesticide container. Make sure that you follow the precautions shown on the product label and work in line with any instructions given on the label or in the relevant notices of approval.

Even when the product label does not say you need to wear PPE, it is good practice for you to wear basic PPE (such as overalls, suitable protective gloves and boots) at all times when handling pesticides or their containers.

All pesticides should be handled in a well-ventilated area to avoid any possible build-up of vapours. Avoid sparks and naked flames as some pesticides may present a fire risk. These products will be labelled with the appropriate hazard symbol and risk phrase.

*If you handle flammable products you should read and understand HSE Guidance booklet HS (G) 51 'The storage of flammable liquids in containers'.*

If pesticide containers are damaged, you will need to take extra precautions.

↘ Wear the PPE stated on the product label or, if this section of the label cannot be read, the appropriate PPE specified in annex E and also that specified on the MSDS.

↘ Immediately contain any spillage and dispose of any contaminated material safely and legally.

If you cannot safely use the contents immediately, either put the damaged container with its contents in another suitable container or transfer the contents to an undamaged container which has held the same product. Whichever alternative you choose, the container must be clearly labelled with the name of the pesticide, information on possible dangers and the precautions to be taken. Where possible, use original labels. Your supplier should be able to help with this or you may be able to get a label from the manufacturer's website.

**Never use an empty food or drink container to hold a pesticide.**

Take care when moving pesticide containers in and out of the store and never leave pesticide containers unattended unless they are in a secure store.

NEVER USE AN EMPTY FOOD OR DRINK CONTAINER TO HOLD A PESTICIDE.

WORKING

## **4.4** TRANSPORTING PESTICIDES

*You can get general guidance on how to meet the legal obligations for transporting dangerous goods in 'Working with ADR, an introduction to the carriage of dangerous goods by road', available from the Department for Transport (you can download this from the Department for Transport website at (www.dft.gov.uk/stellent/groups/ dft_transsec/documents/downloadable/dft_transsec_029427.pdf).*

*The obligations and recommendations for transporting pesticides safely and legally are summarised in 'The carriage of agrochemicals by road: guidance for the agrochemicals industry' published by BASIS (Registration) Ltd. 4.4 Transporting pesticides*

### 4.4.1 THE LAW

This section gives guidance on how to transport pesticides safely and meet the laws relating to carrying dangerous goods (see annex A). Most of the legal conditions only apply above certain amounts which depend on how the goods are being transported (for example, in packages, in tanks or in bulk) as well as on their transport category which may be given in The Carriage of Dangerous Goods and Use of Transportable Pressure Equipment Regulations 2004 as amended (see annex A). Pesticides approved for agricultural use (see annex C) or plant-protection products (but not sulphuric acid) do not have to meet some of these legal conditions as long as they:

↘ have been approved under the Control of Pesticides Regulations 1986 (as amended) or under the Plant Protection Products (Scotland) Regulations 2005;

↘ are transported in or on an agricultural vehicle (see annex C) or any associated trailer;

↘ are diluted ready for use, or supplied in a ready-to-use form; and

↘ are being carried from one piece of agricultural land to another within a 50-kilometre radius.

Although transporting pesticide (especially on farms and holdings) will usually meet these conditions, users collecting pesticides from their suppliers or transporting pesticides from their store to other locations (such as contractors, especially in amenity and forestry areas) may not (depending on the type of vehicle being used and the amount of pesticide being transported).

Even if the exemptions above apply, you may still have to meet other conditions applying to transporting dangerous goods, such as the suitability of vehicles and containers for certain dangerous goods. You should check the relevant laws and guidance carefully.

### 4.4.2 GENERAL PRECAUTIONS WHEN TRANSPORTING PESTICIDES

By following this guidance, you can keep the risk of spillage or similar incidents as low as possible and, if these incidents do occur, make it easier for the emergency services, and other agencies, to deal with them.

Drivers of tractors, vehicles which tow trailers and crop-protection equipment will need to check that coupling pins and other fastening devices are secure before moving off. Anyone involved in transporting pesticides will need to know the procedures to follow if there is an emergency.

If there is a spillage and a possibility of a risk to other people, animals or the environment, take immediate action to limit the effects (for example, to contain the spill). You should also warn others who may be affected or who have an interest (for example, the Scottish Environment Protection Agency).

To protect water from the risks of pesticide pollution, avoid going through water at all times. Wherever possible, avoid crossing watercourses at all. If you cannot avoid water, use a bridge or tunnel.

If a fire breaks out, call the fire brigade, the police and the Scottish Environment Protection Agency. You should give them the relevant information about the type and amount of pesticide involved.

Ask the pesticide manufacturer or fire authority for advice on suitable fire extinguishers. Any run-off from putting out the fire could contain high levels of pesticides and so could be as dangerous and polluting as a spillage.

If a pesticide is transported in equipment used to apply it, make sure that there are no leaks or spills. Maintain hoses, nozzles and other fittings in line with the manufacturer's instructions. Make sure that valves which control the flow of pesticide to the spraying equipment are shut during transport to reduce the risk of leaks and drips. Make sure all covers on equipment are securely closed after tanks or hoppers have been filled.

Take care not to overfill equipment as this may cause the contents to spill during transport, especially over rough ground. This could lead to people and the environment being contaminated.

Pesticides which need to be continually stirred should, whenever possible, be added to the sprayer tank at a suitable area close to the site you are going to treat. This is to avoid the need to have the sprayer pump and recirculating system on while the pesticide is being transported.

You should not transport pesticides with children, animals, farm produce or animal feed. When you need to transport mixed loads, separate them appropriately.

### 4.4.3 TRANSPORTING PESTICIDES INSIDE A VEHICLE

When you are transporting pesticide containers and equipment inside vehicles, keep them separate from the driver and any passengers by a chemical and vapour-proof barrier. Hand-held equipment should be transported empty when possible to avoid the risk of spillage.

To prevent containers being damaged, do not carry them in tractor cabs, tool boxes or in other ways which might lead to them being crushed or punctured.

Secure, leak-proof chests suitable for transporting pesticides are available and you should use one if you are carrying a small quantity of pesticides inside your vehicle.

WORKING

### 4.4.4 LOADING AND UNLOADING PESTICIDES

Take care to prevent damage to pesticide containers and associated equipment when loading or unloading trailers or vehicles. In particular, check whether:

- the containers are stacked as recommended by the manufacturer;

- the trailer needs to have side boards fitted;

- the containers can move about (if so, consider restraining them or putting them in any storage facilities fitted to the vehicle);

- the packaging and label need to be protected from the weather (for example, if they are made of cardboard or paper); and

- machinery is needed or recommended for handling any of the containers (the product label may advise you to use machinery for containers that hold more than 20 litres or weigh more than 25 kilograms).

### 4.4.5 FURTHER ACTION

After use, thoroughly clean equipment which pesticides have been moved or transported in (including contaminated vehicles), and dispose of the washings in a safe and legal way.

## 4.5 FILLING EQUIPMENT

### 4.5.1 WHERE SHOULD I FILL THE EQUIPMENT USED TO APPLY PESTICIDES?

You should carry out all mixing, filling or loading well away from watercourses, ditches and drains. On farms and holdings it is best to have a specific area for filling all sprayers, but when applying pesticides in other forms (for example, as granules or pellets) it is often necessary to load the equipment in the field. Similarly, in many amenity and forestry areas, where work is carried out at several separate locations, it will be necessary to mix and load pesticides at the site. Whenever you carry out mixing, filling or loading you should make sure that you follow the guidance in this code to prevent pollution of surface water and groundwater.

### 4.5.2 WHAT PRECAUTIONS SHOULD I TAKE WHEN FILLING EQUIPMENT?

You must always follow the instructions on the product label when mixing and loading a pesticide into equipment. You should also take the precautions referred to in table 5.

TABLE 5 Action when filling equipment

| Do: | Do not: |
|------|---------|
| use a drip tray to catch any spills and return them to the equipment | use any filling area where the surface is difficult to clean or where small spills are likely to go unnoticed |
| use the foil cutter supplied with the container (or a suitable tool used only for this purpose) to remove secondary seals on containers | use your fingers to break the seal on a container |
| follow the instructions on the product label when opening containers designed for use with a closed-transfer system (see annex C, glossary 1) | try to remove valves and other fittings on returnable containers to remove residual product (these containers are designed and filled to allow for residual product) |
| | (Removing seals which show signs of being opened before is unsafe and may result in extra charges.) |
| re-seal partly-used containers | open more than one container at a time |
| make sure pesticides cannot run back or be drawn back into any water supply | make a direct connection between any water supply and a spray tank |
| use an intermediate tanker or system to prevent pesticide being drawn back | take water straight from a stream, other watercourse or pond into equipment |
| pay close attention to the level of the tank contents when filling (you may find it helpful to use a fill-level alarm, flow meter or pre-set shut-off valve) | leave the sprayer unattended while filling or allow the tank to overflow or to be overfilled |
| take care when filling equipment with a narrow filler opening (such as some backpacks for use with spot guns and CDA lances). Use a suitable funnel and fill slowly | contaminate the outside of hand-held equipment or knapsack sprayers when filling, as this will result in you being contaminated |
| use the appropriate size of pesticide container to reduce the need for measuring or weighing | transfer pesticides between containers, measuring equipment and equipment unless you have to |
| use pesticides in water-soluble packaging where appropriate | try to open water-soluble bags |
| measure out pesticides accurately using suitable equipment used only for this purpose, rinse it immediately and add rinsings to the sprayer. For pesticides which need to be weighed, use scales dedicated to the task | use measuring and dispensing equipment (for example, jugs, buckets and drum pumps) which is used for products other than pesticides |

WORKING

TABLE 5 Action when filling equipment

| Do: | Do not: |
| --- | --- |
| transfer pesticides from small-volume returnable (SVR) containers and intermediate bulk containers (IBC) directly to the equipment using a compatible closed-transfer and measuring system or directly to the pesticide container's built-in transfer device | try to use incompatible transfer equipment, use gravity discharge (flowing out without pumping) from an IBC or transfer a pesticide from a bulk container into smaller containers |
| make sure you are steady on your feet if you have to pour directly into a tank, preferably on the ground or a platform at the right height | lift containers above shoulder height |
| use machinery for handling containers if the product label advises this | try to shake large containers before use (the label will provide guidance on how the product should be stirred or re-circulated before use) |
| use filling devices such as low-level induction bowls or separate mixing hoppers | climb up a sprayer with an open container |
| use a mechanical rinsing device to rinse containers (and contaminated closures and foil seals) if you can, or manually rinse three times (each time using a volume of rinse water equivalent to 10% to 20% of the volume of the container) | try to rinse non-washable non-returnable packaging, returnable containers not intended for rinsing or packaging which has held gassing powders |
| pour slowly, with the container opening positioned so that air can enter while you are pouring (take extra care with narrow-necked containers) | cause glugging |
| put the rinsed foil seal inside each rinsed and drained container or use a single container to collect all the foil seals for rinsing and draining | drop or throw foil seals on the ground |
| replace caps on containers after rinsing and draining and store them upright in an outer carton | leave empty containers upside down to drain on the ground |
| avoid foaming by using appropriate induction, stirring or recirculating systems, and fixing any leaks in the suction system. Use an antifoam or defoamer if necessary | cause foaming by sucking air into the induction system, shaking or stirring the product too much, or adding products likely to foam too early when filling the sprayer |

4

| Do: | Do not: |
|---|---|
| make sure valves are correctly re-set after using an induction bowl or other filling device | let the tank contents flow out through the induction bowl or other filling device if the pump is turned off |
| if mixing two or more pesticides together, follow the correct procedure. Add them to water separately (except where this is not possible for some 'twin-pack' products) and in the recommended order | mix two or more concentrates before or at the same time as loading them into the tank |
| if pesticides will be applied with other chemicals, follow the instructions on the labels of all the relevant products, and use all the information provided by the supplier | pre-mix a pesticide concentrate with an adjuvant, carrier, marker or any other material if this is not allowed under the approved conditions of use of the pesticide and unless an appropriate COSHH assessment has been carried out |
| measure out powder and fine granules in sheltered conditions | let fine particles blow away |
| make sure that the person applying the pesticide has read and understood the product label (and ideally has a copy) if a different person is mixing and loading it | prepare spray solution in bulk for more than one user unless it will be applied using equipment that does not need to be altered to suit individual users (such as stump treatment bottles and spot guns) and does not need to be stirred or shaken constantly |
| have a spill kit available at all times, know how to use it and what other action to take if there is a spillage | try to hose down any spillage |

WORKING

When mixing and loading pesticides, it is illegal (and may be unsafe) to:

↘ mix two or more pesticides which are anticholinesterase compounds (this will be shown on the product labels), unless the mixture is allowed under the approved conditions of use (as shown on the product label of at least one of the pesticides); or

↘ use a pesticide with an adjuvant (a substance that makes the pesticide more effective) unless the adjuvant appears on the authorised list (you can get details from the PSD website at (www.pesticides.gov. uk), and using the pesticide with the adjuvant is in line with both the approved conditions of use for the pesticide and the authorised use of the adjuvant with that pesticide.

If you are applying a pesticide as part of a tank mix, check the following:

↘ That the products are compatible (refer to the compatibility information on the product label and, if necessary, get further guidance from your adviser, supplier or the product's manufacturers);

↘ That the intended volume of water and the spray quality are in line with the recommendations for each product, and all other conditions of use for the individual products (such as application timings) are being met;

↘ That your protection (engineering controls and PPE) reflect the highest obligations stated on the product labels and, where appropriate, any extra needs resulting from your COSHH assessment;

↘ That your measures to protect wildlife and the environment (such as buffer zones) reflect the highest obligations stated on the product labels and, where appropriate, any extra needs resulting from your environmental risk assessment;

↘ That you add the products, one by one, to the spray solution in the order recommended on the label product labels and taking account of any specific mixing instructions (such as amount of water in the tank when each product is added and the stirring or shaking needed); and

↘ That you watch out for any increased risk of foaming or blockage of nozzles and filters.

If a product label does not give guidance on the appropriate order of adding the products to the spray solution when tank mixing, you should add different types of product (as shown on the labels) in the following order.

↘ First add water-soluble bags; then

↘ water-dispersible granules (or soluble granules); then

↘ wettable powders (or soluble powders); then

↘ suspension concentrates; then

↘ emulsifiable concentrates (or oil in water emulsions); and finally

↘ adjuvants.

IF SPRAYER CONTRACTORS ARE USED, IT IS ADVISABLE FOR THEM TO BE REGISTERED WITH THE NATIONAL REGISTER OF SPRAYER OPERATORS (NROSO).

## 4.6 METHODS OF APPLYING PESTICIDE

### 4.6.1 CHOOSING A METHOD

You must use pesticides in line with the conditions of the product approval as stated on the label. For approved uses not specified on the label you must also follow the conditions given on the relevant notice of approval. Unless these documents place a legal obligation on you to use, or not to use, a specific type of equipment to apply the pesticide, you may apply the product using methods other than those recommended as long as:

↘ the equipment you have chosen is suitable for the intended method of applying the pesticide;

↘ the COSHH assessment, where appropriate, has shown that the proposed method does not involve an increased risk to health or safety compared to the normal method;

↘ you have assessed the environmental effects of your intended method of applying the pesticide and your assessment shows there is no increased risk to wildlife or the environment; and

↘ the necessary control measures are in place to reduce, as far as is reasonably possible, the risks to people, wildlife and the environment.

A glossary of the most common terms used to identify equipment for and methods of applying pesticide is at annex C. Remember, in certain circumstances you will need a certificate of competence which is relevant to the application method you are going to use, unless you are working directly under the supervision of a person holding the relevant certificate.

Note: If sprayer contractors are used, it is advisable for them to be registered with the National Register of Sprayer Operators (NRoSO).

### 4.6.2 HOW YOU SHOULD APPLY THE PESTICIDE TO THE AREA TO BE TREATED

Before you begin to apply the pesticide you should consider the order in which you are going to treat the area. You should make sure that you:

↘ do not have to walk, drive or travel through the newly treated crop or area so that you do not contaminate yourself or your equipment; and

↘ leave an untreated or under-dosed area for cleaning the equipment and disposing of sprayer washings.

By treating turning areas and access routes to the treated area last, you will help to make sure that:

↘ you do not contaminate your equipment by travelling through newly treated areas or carrying contaminated soil out of the treated area; and

↘ you and other people can leave and re-enter the area being treated without being contaminated if machinery breaks down, or there is an emergency or other incident which interrupts the work.

### 4.6.3 WHICH APPLICATION METHODS NEED SPECIAL PRECAUTIONS?

The special precautions you need to take depend on the application methods you are using. These precautions will be stated on the product label (and for off-label uses on the notice of approval), when these methods of application are recommended. Some of these application methods are listed in the following paragraphs.

'Reduced-volume spraying' is where the concentrate being sprayed is diluted with a lower volume of water than the minimum volume recommended on the label for that dose. This guidance does not apply to:

⬐ application as fogs and mists;

⬐ use as a concentrated solution through weed wipers;

⬐ approved use of pesticides at low volumes through rotary atomisers, or similar equipment; or

⬐ applying a pesticide concentrate (for example, for some products approved for chemical thinning in forestry).

The application methods listed above should only be used when recommended on the product label.

Using reduced-volume sprays may result in smaller droplet sizes (depending on the type of nozzle used), which may result in an increased risk of drift. Also, if the dose of pesticide is not reduced in the same proportion as the water volume, the more concentrated solution can increase the risk to people and the environment. Because of this, you should make sure that you have taken appropriate action to control drift when considering reduced-volume spraying.

You should not use reduced-volume spraying if the label (or the relevant notice of approval):

⬐ bans reduced-volume spraying (for example, if there is a maximum in-use concentration or minimum application volume); or

⬐ states that PPE must be worn when the product is at the dilution ready for use; or

⬐ has 'corrosive', 'very toxic', 'toxic', or 'risk of serious damage to eyes' on the product label.

In these situations, you may reduce the volume only if you also reduce the dose of product so that the concentration of the spray solution is no greater than that recommended on the product label.

In all other cases you may choose to apply a pesticide as a reduced-volume spray as long as:

⬐ the concentration of the 'reduced-volume' spray is no greater than 10 times the maximum concentration recommended on the label;

⬐ you meet all the conditions of the product approval, including the maximum individual dose of the product;

⬐ you fully understand how to use the spraying equipment and know exactly how to control the spray;

⬐ you use a spray quality no finer than 'fine' for ground-based vehicle-mounted or trailed sprayers and no finer than 'medium' for equipment that is hand controlled;

⬐ you have assessed the risk to human beings (made a COSHH assessment, where appropriate) and the risk to other creatures, plants and the environment (based, where appropriate, on advice from a competent adviser), and made sure that the necessary controls are in place; and

⬐ your protection measures are at least as good as those shown in annex E.

IF YOU ARE USING FOGS, MISTS OR SMOKES IN AN AREA WHERE PEOPLE NORMALLY WORK (FOR EXAMPLE, IN A GLASSHOUSE), YOU MUST MAKE SURE THAT ALL PERSONAL PROPERTY HAS BEEN REMOVED FROM THE AREA BEFORE TREATMENT BEGINS.

### 4.6.5 FOGS, MISTS AND SMOKES IN ENCLOSED SPACES

The reduced-volume spraying advice in 4.6.4 does not apply to these methods of application. Fogs, mists and smoke are treatments normally used in enclosed spaces or indoors, where any possible drift is contained. If you want to use these methods you must meet the label conditions and make your own assessments of risk to human health and the environment. The COSHH assessment must consider the possible risk of breathing in the very small particles or droplets associated with these methods. Fogs (like smoke) use finer particles than mists, and so these stay in the air for considerably longer. If you are not sure whether the equipment you are planning to use is suitable for the relevant method, get advice from the supplier.

If you are using fogs, mists or smokes in an area where people normally work (for example, in a glasshouse), you must make sure that all personal property has been removed from the area before treatment begins. You will also need to make sure that contaminated surfaces (such as unprotected work benches) are thoroughly cleaned after the treatment. It is especially important to remember these precautions when you are using automatic glasshouse misting equipment which works overnight.

Make sure that nobody is in part of the building or structure being treated when you are using dangerous chemicals in these forms, particularly smokes. Check that adequate notices are clearly displayed, especially at all entry points, to stop people entering the area. Make sure that all entrances are secured throughout the treatment period.

Consider where any smoke, drifting particles or vapour from the treatment will end up (for example, by penetrating to another part of the building). Make sure that nobody goes into the building unnecessarily by checking that any items people may need (for example, tools) are removed from the building before treatment. Assess the risks to humans and the environment which might arise from any smoke, particles or vapour escaping, and make sure that the treated area is adequately ventilated before anyone goes back into it. The ventilation method will need to be safe (for example, sending an unprotected worker into the building to open windows would not normally be acceptable).

### 4.6.6 FUMIGANTS

Fumigation is a very specialised task. Because of the nature of fumigants and the risks associated with using them, no-one should carry out fumigation work until they have received proper training. Any fumigation has to be properly planned to prevent the fumigant spreading beyond the area to be treated. You can find guidance on the correct use of fumigants in the HSE guidance document HSG251.

WORKING

# BEFORE USING DUSTS, GRANULES, PELLETS AND BAITS IN AREAS THAT MEMBERS OF THE PUBLIC HAVE ACCESS TO, ASSESS THE RISKS OF ACCIDENTAL EXPOSURE AND USE APPROPRIATE CONTROLS.

### 4.6.7 DUSTS, GRANULES, PELLETS AND BAITS

When using pesticides in the form of a dust, apply them only in suitable conditions and take care to avoid breathing in dust or allowing your skin to become contaminated. Take similar precautions when handling and applying fine granules or granules that give rise to a dust which may be dangerous. You will need to take extra care when applying these products by hand (if allowed) or hand-held equipment. Pesticide which some granules release as a vapour (especially in warm conditions) may also be dangerous, particularly in confined spaces. It is important to follow all instructions on product labels and make sure that you use appropriate equipment to apply the pesticide. Clear up and safely dispose of spilt granules or baits. If it is recommended, make sure that granules are incorporated into the soil, compost or so on correctly and within the time specified.

Slug pellets can present a significant risk to wildlife and pets. You can reduce this risk by:

↘ drilling pellets with seed, if this is appropriate and recommended on the product label;

↘ applying them at the correct rate;

↘ clearing up spillages (pellets or pellet and seeds mixed) immediately;

↘ never leaving packs of slug pellets unattended and not storing slug pellets mixed with seed; and

↘ checking your field before you leave it to make sure there is no risk to animals, people or other creatures.

Inadequately protected baits for vertebrate control and the carcasses of pests can be dangerous to wildlife and pets. Make sure that you protect baits to prevent access by other species, remove the bait after use and search for carcasses so you can dispose of them safely and legally.

Wildlife and domestic animals may be put at risk during test-baiting to check how severe a pest problem is. When test-baiting, make sure that you adequately protect the baits to prevent poisoning creatures you did not intend to treat.

Before using these products in areas that members of the public have access to, assess the risks of accidental exposure and use appropriate controls.

In all situations, take every precaution to avoid spillages (and to completely clean up any that do occur) and overdosing in a particular area.

Take care when you are cleaning equipment designed for applying dusts, pellets or granules. If possible, do not use air lines and take care when brushing to prevent the substance contaminating the air.

### 4.6.8 USING VEHICLES WITHOUT CABS

Spraying from vehicles without cabs may result in a high level of exposure through your skin or by breathing in the spray. You should take care to keep your exposure to spray drift as low as possible and you must wear appropriate PPE (possibly as well as that specified on the product label).

Similarly, using a vehicle without a cab to apply slug pellets and granules may result in high levels of exposure, especially when the product is dusty or dust is created during the application. You must carry out an appropriate COSHH assessment to identify how to avoid or control exposure.

*You can get more guidance on spraying from vehicles without cabs in the HSE Agriculture Information Sheet 33 'Safe use of all-terrain vehicles (ATVs) in agriculture and forestry'. This is on the HSE website (www.hse.gov.uk/pubns/ais33.pdf).*

IF YOU ARE APPLYING A PESTICIDE WHICH HAS BEEN PREPARED BY ANOTHER PERSON, MAKE SURE THAT YOU HAVE READ AND UNDERSTOOD THE PRODUCT LABEL.

### 4.6.9 PAVED AREAS AND PUBLIC FOOTPATHS

Applying pesticides on hard surfaces may lead to run-off and you should take extra care to make sure that pesticides do not enter drains or watercourses. Run-off can also pollute groundwater.

Before you use a vehicle to apply a pesticide on a footpath, consult the local authority and, if necessary, get their permission. When choosing the product and how to apply it, remember that people and animals are likely to be using the footpath. Always drive the vehicle at a speed which is appropriate for the work being done, the local conditions and the safety of people in the area. Be prepared to stop if necessary.

### 4.6.10 USING HAND-HELD EQUIPMENT

When using hand-held equipment, you should try to avoid contaminating yourself by walking through the crop or area you have just treated, especially when you are working in a high crop. Avoid working into the wind when you are spraying or applying dusts and fine granules by hand or using hand-held equipment.

When using a knapsack sprayer, you must take care to achieve the intended application rate and to prevent spray drifting off target. Using a suitable spray pressure control valve and nozzle cover may help.

When filling equipment, be careful:

- not to allow the outside of any backpack used with a controlled droplet application (CDA) lance or spot gun to become contaminated (special care needs to be taken when filling narrow-necked backpacks);

- to avoid overfilling the spray tank;

- to make sure that you replace the filler cap correctly and firmly; and

- to prevent spillage (for example, by filling equipment within a portable drip tray or a 'bunded area' sealed off from the ground with raised edges).

Do not prepare a spray solution in bulk for several users unless the equipment you are using does not need to be adjusted to suit individual users (for example, where a dilution rate is stated only for knapsack sprayers).

If you are applying a pesticide which has been prepared by another person, make sure that you have read and understood the product label.

You should not use hand-held equipment while driving any vehicle.

WORKING

## IF POSSIBLE, DO NOT REMOVE DRY OR DUSTY DEPOSITS USING AIR LINES AND TAKE CARE WHEN BRUSHING TO PREVENT THE DUST BEING CARRIED IN THE AIR.

### 4.6.11 SEED TREATMENTS

If you are using mobile seed-treatment equipment you should make sure that the seed-treatment product is supplied in containers which are not too large to be carried, handled and used safely.

Take care when you are cleaning seed-treatment or seed-drilling equipment. If possible, do not remove dry or dusty deposits using air lines and take care when brushing to prevent the dust being carried in the air.

Some seed treatments leave a dusty deposit on the seed and a residue in the seed container and drilling equipment. Be careful to avoid breathing in the dust or contaminating your skin, especially when handling treated seed, setting equipment and cleaning equipment after use. Dispose of seed bags, other contaminated material and unused treated seed safely and take care to avoid contaminating people or the environment. Make sure that all the treated seeds you plant are completely covered with the appropriate depth of soil and, if you spill any treated seed, clear it up straight away.

### 4.6.12 DIPPING AND DRENCHING TREATMENTS

Using pesticides as a dip or a drench may result in high levels of skin contamination from splashes, run-off from the freshly treated material and contact with contaminated debris when cleaning the equipment. Breathing in pesticide vapour may also be a problem when dipping and drenching. Make sure there is good ventilation for people applying the product, handling the treated material or working in contaminated areas. Follow the conditions on the product label (see also annex E).

Where possible, avoid dipping by hand and make full use of equipment which will reduce your exposure during the treatment process and result in the lowest possible amount of run-off from treated material (for example, using an electrostatic spraying booth for forestry transplants or using foam treatment equipment for onion sets). Using this equipment will also reduce the environmental problems associated with making too much pesticide solution and run-off from freshly treated material.

Always dispose of used or extra pesticide mixtures and unused treated material safely and legally. Make sure that treated material is labelled and not left unattended. When carrying out your COSHH and environmental-risk assessments, remember that workers who plant treated material or handle treated produce may not know what pesticides have been used or the precautions they should take as a result.

### 4.6.13 WEED CONTROL IN OR NEAR WATER

Very few pesticides are approved for use in or near water and you must consult the Scottish Environment Protection Agency before using a pesticide in these situations. Before using a pesticide in water or in areas immediately next to watercourses, you must have had relevant training and, where appropriate, you must have any certificates of competence for the way you will be applying the pesticide in these situations.

### 4.6.14 APPLYING PESTICIDES FROM AN AIRCRAFT

The various legal obligations and general obligations relating to applying pesticides from the air are explained in annex G.

## 4.7 SPRAY DRIFT

### 4.7.1 THE EFFECTS OF SPRAY DRIFT

By law, pesticides must only be applied to the land, crop, structure, material or other area you are treating. Spray drifting off target is a common result of misusing pesticides and causes problems between pesticide users and their neighbours.

Spray drift can also cause damage to the environment and wildlife (both on land and in water) and result in water pollution. In some cases, spraying may be illegal if you do not follow the proper procedures for consulting and giving notice to the Scottish Environment Protection Agency and Scottish Natural Heritage.

Remember, pesticides applied as dust or fine granules can also drift. You must take care to apply these products in suitable weather conditions with suitable equipment, correctly adjusted for the product you are using.

### 4.7.2 WHAT CAUSES SPRAY DRIFT?

A combination of factors may contribute to spray drift, including:

- the speed of the wind;

- the height of the spray nozzles, the design of the equipment and ground conditions;

- the spray quality (which will depend on the choice of nozzles and the spray pressure);

- the type of crop or other vegetation, if any;

- the speed of the vehicle the spray is being applied from;

- local atmospheric conditions;

- the condition of the equipment used to apply the pesticide; and

- the equipment settings.

WORKING

### 4.7.3 WEATHER CONDITIONS

Do not apply pesticides in a way which may lead to drift. Issues to think about:

⬊ if the wind direction and speed would cause the pesticide to drift away from the target; or

⬊ if there is a chance that air movement will carry spray droplets or vapour away from the target area.

This is especially important when spraying near sensitive areas.

Check the weather forecast before starting work. The Meteorological Office gives information on wind speed measured at 10 metres above the ground. When spraying a typical field crop or grassland, the wind speed at the correct height of the nozzle (an important factor affecting drift) will be roughly half the value measured at 10 metres. If there is no crop (for example, when spraying hard surfaces in amenity areas) the wind speed at the height of the nozzle may be more than half of the value at 10 metres above the ground. As wind speed and direction will be influenced by a variety of local factors (such as the presence of trees and buildings), it is important to assess the suitability of the conditions at the area you intend to treat.

When you arrive at the area you intend to treat, look for signs to show you the wind speed and direction. If you have a suitable wind-speed meter (anemometer), use this. However, you should take care to make sure that individual meter readings reflect the general situation as you see it.

Remember that hot, dry weather will reduce the size of spray droplets because of evaporation and increase the risk of spray drift.

The safest conditions in which to spray are when it is cool and humid with a steady wind of 2 to 4 miles an hour or 3.2 to 6.5 kilometres an hour (light breeze) blowing away from any sensitive areas or neighbours' land. Avoid spraying in the following weather conditions:

⬊ when there is little or no wind under a clear sky in the morning or evening, when air layers do not mix, as any drift may hang over the treated area and unexpected air movements may move it to other places;

⬊ when there are low winds on warm sunny afternoons when humidity is low; and

⬊ when temperatures are above 30°C, as rising air currents may carry spray droplets and vapour in an unexpected way.

Whatever equipment you use, make sure that you do not use it when the wind will cause the pesticide to drift off target. In general, if you have low-drift spraying equipment, use this to improve the targeting of your pesticide and reduce (to the lowest possible level) the environmental effect.

Table 6 is a guide to assessing wind speed and recommendations for standard field crop sprayers. The relationship between the wind speed at the height of the spray nozzles and the wind speed (according to the Beaufort scale, measured at a height of 10 metres above the ground) assumes that there is a crop covering the ground. If there is no crop or grass cover, the wind speed at the height of the spray nozzle will be higher.

TABLE 6 A guide to wind speed and using field-crop sprayers with conventional nozzles

| Beaufort scale (measured 10 metres above the ground) | Description | Visible signs | Guide for using a standard crop sprayer | Approximate wind speed at the height of the spray nozzle |
|---|---|---|---|---|
| Force 0 | Calm | Smoke rises vertically | Use only 'medium' or 'coarse' spray quality | Less than 2 kilometres an hour (less than 1.2 miles an hour) |
| Force 1 | Light air | Smoke drifts, showing the wind direction | Acceptable spraying conditions | 2 to 3.2 kilometres an hour (1.2 to 2 miles an hour) |
| Force 2 | Light breeze | Leaves rustle and you can feel the wind on your face | Ideal spraying conditions | 3.2 to 6.5 kilometres an hour (2 to 4 miles an hour) |
| Force 3 | Gentle breeze | Leaves and twigs are constantly moving | Increased risk of spray drift. Avoid spraying herbicides and take special care with other pesticides | 6.5 to 9.6 kilometres an hour (4 to 6 miles an hour) |
| Force 4 | Moderate breeze | Small branches are moved and dust and loose paper are raised | Do not spray | 9.6 to 14.5 kilometres an hour (6 to 9 miles an hour) |

WORKING

## 4.7.4 HOW CAN OFF-TARGET DRIFT BE PREVENTED OR CONTROLLED?

When using pesticides, take all reasonable precautions to prevent drifting off target. Reasonable precautions include using appropriate methods and equipment to apply the product, taking account of the weather conditions, taking account of neighbours' interests and protecting members of the public, wildlife and the environment. Consider the following points:

⬎ Check the weather forecast and the conditions at the site you are treating before you start to apply a pesticide. Do not apply a pesticide if it is likely to drift off target or if there is a chance that wind will carry spray droplets or vapour away from the target area;

⬎ Reducing the dose of the product you apply will reduce the amount of product which will drift off target;

⬎ Use the coarsest appropriate spray quality at all times;

⬎ When using a sprayer, keep the boom as low as possible, providing an even spray pattern at the correct target height. The correct boom height will depend on the spray pattern and the angle of the individual nozzles, the space between nozzles, the flatness of the area being treated and the design of the boom;

⬎ When using a sprayer with hydraulic nozzles, reduce the spray pressure and speed of the vehicle (but make sure you maintain the intended dose, water volume and spray quality);

⬎ Consider not treating an area closest to the downwind border of the area you are treating. For field crops, an untreated buffer zone will be most effective if the crop (or plants of at least the same height as the crop) continues into the buffer zone;

⬎ In orchards, consider having appropriate natural windbreaks, such as other trees, around the treated area;

⬎ Use one of the various spraying systems which are available to help reduce spray drift. Suitable drift-reducing systems may include twin-fluid nozzles, air-induction nozzles, rotary atomisers, pre-orifice nozzles, air-assistance for field crop sprayers, shrouded-boom sprayers for sports turf and other amenity areas, and re-circulating tunnel sprayers for spraying fruit bushes and trees. Sprayers and nozzles meeting the needs for low-drift equipment under the LERAP schemes will give lower levels of drift than conventional systems when used correctly; and

⬎ Use an authorised drift-reducing additive to pesticides in appropriate situations (depending on the type of equipment being used and the nature of the spray solution).

*Pesticide manufacturers and suppliers will be able to give you information on their nozzles and spraying systems.*

*You can get general advice on how to choose nozzles which will apply the pesticide effectively while reducing drift in the Voluntary Initiative stewardship leaflet 'Nozzle selection and maintenance', which includes the Home Grown Cereals Authority (HGCA) nozzle selection chart (see www.voluntaryinitiative.org.uk).*

*You may wish to be aware of TIBRE, an initiative by Scottish Natural Heritage which aims to show how technology can be used in farming to benefit the environment while maintaining business profitability.*

## 4.8 AFTER WORKING WITH PESTICIDES

### 4.8.1 WHAT YOU NEED TO DO AFTER YOU HAVE APPLIED A PESTICIDE

The following is a brief checklist of what you need to do when you have finished applying a pesticide.

✓ Clean the equipment you have used, inside and out, preferably before leaving the treatment area. Dispose of unused spray solution and sprayer washings safely and legally. The cleaning area should not be close to surface water, drainage channels or any sensitive terrestrial habitat.

✓ After cleaning, store the sprayer (or other equipment) under cover.

✓ Return any unused pesticide concentrate to your pesticide store.

✓ Keep the appropriate records.

✓ Remove warning notices when they are no longer needed.

✓ If you have given warnings to beekeepers, tell them that you have finished applying the pesticide.

✓ Make sure that you:

  ↘ dispose of used PPE safely and legally (if it is not designed to be used again or is unfit for further use); or

  ↘ where appropriate, clean re-usable PPE before you store it and dispose of washings safely and legally; and

  ↘ report any faults with engineering controls or PPE.

✓ Let the appropriate manufacturers know (either directly or through the supplier) if you have found any product-related, packaging-related or equipment-related problems when mixing, loading or applying the product.

# DISPOSING OF PESTICIDE WASTE

This part of the code gives guidance on handling and disposing of pesticide waste (including concentrates, ready-to-use formulations and pesticide solutions), contaminated material and equipment and pesticide packaging.

The Scottish Executive has brought in regulations that apply to waste from agricultural premises (see 'The Waste (Scotland) Regulations 2005' in          ). These regulations, which came into force on 21 January 2005, place similar restrictions on farmers, crofters and growers to those that already apply in amenity and forestry areas. If you cause any pollution of air, water or soil, you can be prosecuted. Farmers, crofters and growers should follow the guidance in this code to make sure they dispose of waste pesticides in a safe and legal way to keep any unwanted effect on the environment or humans as low as possible.

If you reduce your use of pesticides, you will also reduce the amount of waste pesticide and empty containers you produce, and you will save money. You should consider the following questions.

Do you need to use the pesticide and, if you do, can you reduce its use?

Do you have suitable pesticides currently in stock and can you order less new stock?

Have you chosen the most suitable pack sizes?

Can you manage and control the use of pesticides any better?

Can you use any of the following methods to reduce packaging waste and reduce the washings produced?

- Soluble packs

- Returnable containers

- Closed-transfer systems

- Flushing systems for low-volume sprayers

- Direct-injection systems

- Rounding down your calculations of the amount of pesticide needed when filling your sprayer to allow you to dispose of the washings on an under-dosed area (or using a suitable electronic sprayer controller to achieve the same result)

Will your contractor or distributor take back properly cleaned (using a pressure rinsing device or manually rinsed at least three times) empty containers?

DISPOSAL

Whenever possible, use up pesticides in the approved way. When a product's approval has been withdrawn or amended for commercial, safety or other reasons, a 'wind-down' period is given to allow remaining stocks of the product to be used up. The only exception is where there are major safety concerns. The PSD website at https://secure.pesticides.gov.uk/pestreg/ gives details of the approval status of individual products and details of reviews which may affect a range of products. By checking this information, or asking your supplier, the manufacturer or an adviser, you should be able to avoid having to dispose of unapproved products.

Similarly, by managing your chemical store properly, you should be able to avoid having to dispose of pesticides because they have deteriorated or because products are out of date.

***You should know about the HSE advice on storing pesticides given in the HSE Guidance Note AS 16 'Guidance on storing pesticides for farmers and other professional users'.***

You should avoid storing an unwanted pesticide, and it is illegal to do so if the approval for storing and using it has been withdrawn.

If a container or other packaging is damaged, but the product is still approved for use, you may be able to carefully transfer the product to the equipment used to apply it, leaving only the container to be disposed of.

Despite good management, you may have some concentrates or ready-to-use pesticides that you need to dispose of. You should never dilute an unwanted concentrate in order to dispose of it as dilute pesticide waste. You should consider the following points.

Firstly, ask your supplier if they will take back any unwanted, unused pesticides that are packaged, labelled and of good quality.

Pesticide concentrates are likely to be 'special waste' (known as 'hazardous waste' in England and Wales) and may present a significant risk to the environment or to humans. Handling and disposing of this type of waste is tightly controlled and you will need to use an authorised carrier who is registered with the Scottish Environment Protection Agency and a licensed waste-disposal contractor. You will be able to find such a contractor in The Phone Book).

You must store unwanted concentrates and ready-to-use formulation in your chemical store to make sure they are secure and that any spills will be contained.

You (or the carrier if you use one), must obtain a 'consignment note' from the Scottish Environment Protection Agency, complete it and give SEPA at least 72 hours prior notice if you intend to move or dispose of 'special waste'. You (as the waste producer) and the people transporting and receiving the waste must keep copies of the consignment notes for at least three years. Also, you must not move 'special waste' until the appropriate period for notice has passed.

When you have filled in the necessary consignment notes, you should pass the unwanted concentrates to a licensed waste-disposal contractor.

As the producer of the waste, you must make sure that the person who takes your waste is authorised to take it and can transport it safely, and that it will be safely disposed of or recycled.

You must also fill in a 'waste transfer note' providing a clear written description of the waste preferably using the appropriate European Waste Catalogue (EWC) codes (the ewc codes can be found on the SEPA website at www.sepa.org.uk/guidance/waste/hazardous/index.htm). You can write this on the transfer note itself. Both you and the waste-disposal contractor must keep copies of the transfer note and written description for two years. If the waste is 'special' and you have filled in a 'consignment note', you do not also need to fill in a 'waste transfer note'.

If you can transport your own unwanted pesticides safely and legally, you can take these to a licensed treatment or disposal site, after checking whether the site will accept your waste.

**If you need more guidance, contact the Scottish Environment Protection Agency.**

For pesticide products which are applied undiluted and without a carrier (for example, ready-to-use formulations, granules, dusts, pellets and baits), you should be able to apply the product with no, or very little, extra product left in the equipment. The general guidance on cleaning application equipment also applies to these types of pesticide, although equipment used for applying solid pesticide is not usually cleaned using water.

'Special' or 'hazardous' waste is defined under the European Hazardous Waste Directive 1991 (see
) and the EU has produced the European Waste Catalogue (EWC) which lists all wastes whether hazardous or not. The EWC also states whether materials that can be dangerous are classified as 'special' or 'hazardous' waste under all circumstances or only when a hazardous substance is present above a certain concentration. You can see the EWC and get guidance on deciding whether your waste is 'special waste' on the Scottish Environment Protection Agency website at www.sepa.org.uk/guidance/waste/hazardous/index.htm or phone your local SEPA office. You will find details of your local SEPA office in the phone book or at www.sepa.org.uk/contact/index.htm.

**You can get more information on hazardous waste from the Chartered Institution of Wastes Management website (www.ciwm.co.uk).**

If you are spraying a pesticide, you should be able to do so with no, or very little, spray solution left over. Planning this will reduce your waste disposal problems and will save you money. However, in other situations (such as when you are applying a pesticide as a before planting or after harvesting dipping treatment) you may not always be able to avoid having dilute pesticide left over at the end of the treatment.

When you are treating several sites, one after another, using the same pesticide and the same equipment, you may be able to use left over spray from one site to treat another, if you can transport the pesticide safely and legally.

You must dispose of all dilute pesticide waste (including any leftover pesticides and all sprayer washings) safely and legally to protect humans, wildlife and the environment, especially groundwater and surface water.

When you have finished applying the pesticide, clean both the inside and the outside of all equipment you have used. By thoroughly cleaning your application equipment, in line with the manufacturer's instructions, you will help to:

➘ reduce any risk from handling contaminated surfaces;

➘ prevent damage to other crops and areas which will be treated later using the same equipment; and

➘ reduce the risk of blockages.

Before cleaning your equipment you should read and follow the label instructions on:

➘ using appropriate PPE when handling contaminated surfaces; and

➘ carrying out any decontamination procedures relating to the particular product (for example, some herbicides need to be de-activated with ammonia-based cleaning agents).

If possible, you should clean the equipment you have used, inside and out, at the site of the treatment. This should be at least 10 metres from watercourses and 50 metres from wells, springs, etc, rather than having a single, dedicated site for cleaning. You should use any built-in rinsing systems that are fitted to clean the inside of the equipment quickly and effectively while using the minimum volume of rinse water. Similarly, a hose and brush attachment which is available on some sprayers and can be fitted to others will help you to clean the outside of the equipment more effectively than a high pressure spray gun, and will use less water. Repeated tank washing, each using a small amount of water, will achieve better results than a single rinse using a large amount of water and will also produce less washings. As well as cleaning the tank, you will also need to make sure that all pipes, hoses, filters, valves, nozzles and induction systems are thoroughly cleaned. All facilities for washing equipment should be designed to make sure that the pesticide solution cannot get into your washing water under any circumstances.

*You can get more guidance on cleaning sprayers on the Voluntary Initiative website (www.voluntaryinitiative.org.uk/Content/Agr_BP.asp)*

*The HSE report 'Exposure to spray residues on agricultural equipment' (HSE 4023.R51.192) provides useful, practical guidance on avoiding contamination on the outside of application equipment (see www.hse.gov.uk/research/crr_htm/2002/crr02440.htm).*

Possible options for disposing of dilute pesticide waste include the following:

You can apply the contaminated water to the treated or untreated crop within the terms of the product approval. But make sure you do not go over the maximum dose.

You can store the contaminated water in a suitable container until a licensed waste-disposal contractor can collect it.

When using pesticides in agriculture, you can only dispose of the dilute waste onto soil or grass either directly or fed by the drainage from a hard surface under the terms of a licence, known as a CAR licence, issued under The Water Environment (Controlled Activities) (Scotland) Regulations 2005 (see          ) by the Scottish Environment Protection Agency. A CAR licence would, if granted, stipulate the terms that must be complied with. The land you choose for this purpose must:

- be able to absorb the volume of liquid to be disposed of onto it without run-off or leaving puddles;

- result in the smallest possible risk to wildlife and watercourses;

- protect groundwater (by not allowing the pesticide to reach the water table);

- present the smallest possible risk to septic tanks, field drains or sewerage systems; and

- where necessary, be signposted and fenced to keep people and livestock out.

If you have suitable equipment such as your own effluent treatment plant designed for treating liquid waste containing pesticides, you can process the dilute waste yourself, as long as:

- you (or the person using the equipment) have appropriate authority under the Waste Management Licensing Regulations (see          );

- the treated effluent is collected and is disposed of as outlined in the appropriate authority under the Waste Management Licensing Regulations (see          ).

You can dispose of the dilute waste to a lined biobed (see the          ) as long as:

- you have appropriate authority under the Waste Management Licensing Regulations (see          );

- the water flowing out from the base of the biobed is collected and is disposed of as outlined in the appropriate authority under the Waste Management Licensing Regulations (see          ).

You can dispose of the dilute waste into a sewer under a 'trade effluent consent' issued by Scottish Water which manages the sewage treatment works the sewer is connected to. Waste that contains substances classified as 'special category effluent' also need approval from the Scottish Environment Protection Agency before a 'trade effluent consent' can be issued.

*You can get more information on the design of, use of, and licensing conditions for biobeds, from the Voluntary Initiative website or your local Scottish Environment Protection Agency office.*

DISPOSAL

Do not reuse an empty pesticide container for any purpose unless:

   it is specifically designed to be returned and refilled and you are doing so in line with the label instructions; or

   you are filling it with an identical pesticide product transferred from a damaged container.

The product label will state whether you should rinse the container after emptying it.

Before disposing of a non-returnable container, make sure it is completely empty.

If you can, containers for products which are concentrates and are applied as a solution should be thoroughly rinsed before being disposed of.

Containers for ready-to-use formulations or products not applied as a solution are normally not rinsed after emptying.

Containers for hydrogen cyanide gassing powders or aluminium, magnesium or zinc phosphides must never be rinsed or cleaned.

Before disposing of rigid, non-returnable containers, you should always thoroughly rinse them in line with the label instructions.

If there are no instructions, you should:

   use purpose-made container-rinsing equipment in line with the manufacturer's instructions (for example, pressure rinsing devices forming part of many sprayer induction bowls); or

rinse containers by hand at least three times (or until the container is visibly clean) with clean water. Add the rinsings to the spray solution.

You may also be able to rinse some types of flexible packaging designed for solid pesticides which are applied as a solution, depending on the material and design of these packs. You should always rinse containers immediately after emptying them, once you have allowed the product to drain fully into the equipment that is applying it. You should also rinse contaminated closures caps and seals and any contamination on the outside of containers. All rinsings should be added to the spray solution.

If, for any reason, you have container rinsings which you cannot add to the application equipment (for example, if you are not applying the pesticide as a spray or dipping solution), you should collect the contaminated rinsings in a suitable, labelled container, and store it in a safe place. You should then dispose of the rinsings in line with the guidance given in            .

Containers which are not suitable for rinsing (for example, paper sacks and cardboard cartons) and those containing products which are either ready-to-use or not applied as a solution, are normally emptied completely but not rinsed. These will have the phrase 'Empty container completely and dispose of safely' on the label. You should handle and store these empty containers as if they still contained the pesticide, and you should dispose of them through a licensed waste-disposal contractor.

You must not rinse or clean empty containers which hydrogen cyanide gassing powders or aluminium, magnesium or zinc phosphides have been supplied in or kept in because of the dangerous gases they give off when they come into contact with moisture. You should handle and store these empty containers as if they still contained the pesticide and you should dispose of them through a licensed waste-disposal contractor.

5

Firmly replace caps on containers immediately after rinsing and draining them into the equipment used for applying pesticide. Put the rinsed foil seal inside the container. Store the rinsed and drained containers upright in a secure, weatherproof area away from stored pesticides (either in a separate store or a separate part of your chemical store), until you can dispose of them.

**You can get more guidance on cleaning containers on the Voluntary Initiative website (www. voluntaryinitiative.org.uk/Content?agr).**

You can dispose of rinsed pesticide containers in the following ways:

Pass them on to a licensed waste-disposal contractor.

Take them to a licensed waste-disposal or waste-recovery site, after checking whether the site will accept rinsed containers.

Burn them only in an incinerator licensed by your local authority or the Scottish Environment Protection Agency. You should contact your local Scottish Environment Protection Agency office for more information if this is your preferred option.

Containers that have been thoroughly rinsed and drained will generally be accepted at licensed waste-disposal sites as long as the conditions of the site operator's licence allow this. The local Scottish Environment Protection Agency office can give you details of these sites.

Do not use empty pesticide containers or contaminated pallets for transporting food or animal feed.

You should arrange to dispose of contaminated packaging, equipment, unwanted protective clothing and waste from dealing with spills and leaks through a licensed waste-disposal contractor. Some of this waste may need to be dealt with as 'special waste'.

You should dispose of used vertebrate control agents, other pesticide baits and carcasses in line with the guidance on the product label. If no advice is given on the label, arrange to dispose of this waste through a licensed waste-disposal contractor, making sure that you follow the correct procedure.

You should dispose of used compost, soil and so on which have been treated with pesticides in line with the guidance on the product label and in accordance with the necessary permissions from SEPA. If no advice is given on the label, get guidance from your local SEPA office. You can also get information on the PSD website (www. pesticides.gov.uk/uploadedfiles/Compost-disposal.pdf).

You should arrange to dispose of other materials such as treated seed, other treated plant material and used crop covers which are contaminated with pesticides through a licensed waste-disposal contractor.

You can get more detailed, up-to-date information on how to dispose of waste resulting from the use of pesticides from the NETREGS website at www.netregs. gov.uk or by contacting your local SEPA office.

DISPOSAL

6

# KEEPING RECORDS

IT IS BEST PRACTICE FOR
YOU TO KEEP A COPY OF
THE CURRENT STOCK LIST
AWAY FROM THE STORE
ITSELF BUT WHERE IT IS
STILL EASY TO GET TO.

## 6.1 RECORD GUIDANCE

This part of the code provides guidance on the different types of records and explains exactly what you need to record and why. The table at the end of this part gives a summary of the records and the reasons for them.

## 6.2 STORAGE RECORDS

You do not have to, but you might find it helpful to keep records of all the contents of your chemical store (for both fixed and mobile stores). These records will:

ⅴ help with stock rotation and control;

ⅴ keep an accurate and up-to-date list of the contents of the chemical store if there is an emergency;

ⅴ help you avoid overstocking;

ⅴ help you to make sure that you do not have any unapproved or unwanted pesticide products; and

ⅴ help you to use up oldest stocks first to avoid deterioration.

It is best practice for you to keep a copy of the current stock list away from the store itself but where it is still easy to get to.

## 6.3 RECORDS OF PESTICIDE TREATMENTS

By law, those who produce food and animal feed must keep records of pesticide treatments. The legislation which demands this is:

ⅴ The Food Hygiene (Scotland) Regulations 2006, (see annex A), which implements EC Regulation 852/2004 on the hygiene of foodstuffs (annex I, part A, III (Record keeping)); and,

ⅴ The Feed (Hygiene and Enforcement) (Scotland) Regulations 2005, (see annex A), which implements EC Regulation 183/2005 on the hygiene of feed for livestock (annex I, part A, II (Record keeping)).

Both came into force in January 2006. They explain that people who produce or harvest plant products for people or animals to eat must keep records of any plant protection products (pesticides) or biocides they use. Other people, such as vets, agronomists and farm technicians, can help you to keep these records.

Other professional users will need to keep records of applications in the future. You should keep these records now as part of good practice.

It has always been very good practice to keep records of all activities involving storing and using pesticides, not just those products applied as a spray. These records are useful to refer to if people, crops in the next field, other creatures or the environment are accidentally contaminated, or if someone claims that contamination has taken place.

Accurate records will also help you meet the terms of any pesticide conditions, such as:

ⅴ the time that needs to pass before harvesting;

ⅴ intervals between repeat applications;

ⅴ periods when livestock cannot go on a treated area; and

ⅴ periods when workers cannot enter treated areas.

KEEPING RECORDS

PSD will publish more guidance on the format you should keep records in and how long you should keep them for. Make sure you can fill them in easily and without mistakes, and that they are understandable and can be read quickly.

Annex F gives a suggested format for a satisfactory treatment record for the time being. These records can be written by hand in a book or entered on a computer. It is better if you do not use loose pages in a binder because pages can be lost.

If you are a member of a crop assurance scheme or the woodland assurance standard, you will need to meet specific conditions for making and keeping treatment records. You also need to keep certain records for LERAPs.

It is good practice to record treatments made to areas close to homes or other properties which a lot of people occupy (such as schools, residential homes, hospitals and so on). You may want to record the date and time, name the pesticide used (including the MAPP number), refer to any environmental or COSHH assessment made, refer to any notice given to the area or signs set up (including when they were put up and taken down) and so on. You may also want to keep a record of any questions you receive from your neighbours.

If someone suggests that they may have been affected by a pesticide, it is important to give them, their advisers or the HSE full and accurate information as soon as possible (including the full name of the product with its MAPP number, any other information such as risk and safety phrases and medical information). This information will normally be shown on the product label.

It is best if you make sure you keep your records to hand in your farm or local office. Information is then easy to get to and not just kept by suppliers, contractors or advisers. When you use a contractor, they should make and keep records on applying the pesticide and, as the owner or occupier of the treated land or local treatment manager for the local authority or other treated area, you should ask the contractor for a copy of these records.

It is also good practice to assess and record the effectiveness of each pesticide treatment after a suitable time has passed. This information is important in identifying problems with:

- how the pesticide has been applied;

- crop damage (possibly only affecting certain varieties); or

- any resistance pests are building up.

These records can help you to:

- improve application methods and product choice;

- share information with pesticide and equipment manufacturers; and

- supply information to PSD as appropriate.

**You can find information on pesticide resistance and the work of the various resistance action groups on the PSD website (www.pesticides.gov.uk).**

## 6.4 COSHH ASSESSMENT RECORDS

A record of a COSHH assessment, when one is needed, should include:

- the full name of the pesticide (and the relevant HSE or MAPP number);

- the possible risks to health which may result from pesticide being used;

- the steps which you need to take to prevent, or adequately control, exposure in line with COSHH; and

- the other action necessary to meet the obligations of COSHH for example:

    - using and maintaining measures which control exposure;

    - monitoring exposure;

    - health surveillance; and

    - training and instructing those who use pesticides.

You must keep COSHH assessment records readily available.

## 6.5 RECORDS OF ENVIRONMENTAL RISK ASSESSMENTS

A record of any environmental risk assessment should include:

- the name of, and a description of, the pesticide (as for a COSHH assessment record);

- the possible risks to wildlife and the environment which may result from using the pesticide;

- the steps you need to take to prevent, or adequately control, exposure of wildlife and the environment;

- the specific details needed when you apply a pesticide in line with the LERAP schemes, and any other information which may be relevant when you use pesticides in certain situations (for example, when using a pesticide in or near water); and

- details of any nearby springs, wells or boreholes within the treated area, and the action you need to take to prevent contamination of groundwater.

## 6.6 RECORDS OF MONITORING EXPOSURE

In situations where your employer needs to monitor exposure to pesticides, the monitoring records should provide adequate information on:

↘ when your employer carried out the monitoring and what the results were;

↘ what monitoring procedures were used and how long the monitoring periods were; and

↘ the type of samples which were taken, where the samples were taken from, the work in progress at the time and, in the case of samples taken from people, the names of the people being monitored.

## 6.7 MAINTENANCE RECORDS OF EXPOSURE CONTROL MEASURES

Under the COSHH regulations, employers and self-employed people must keep suitable records of inspections and tests of engineering controls and respiratory protective equipment (RPE). A suitable record of each inspection and test of RPE will include:

↘ the name and address of the employer responsible for the RPE;

↘ details of the equipment including any distinguishing number or mark, together with a description that is adequate to identify it, and the name of the maker;

↘ the date of the inspection or test and the name and signature (or unique authentication) of the person who carried it out;

↘ the condition of the equipment and details of any faults found including, in the case of canister or filter respirators, the condition of the canister and filter;

↘ details of any repairs carried out as a result of the inspection or test;

↘ in the case of compressed-air or oxygen apparatus, the pressure of the air or oxygen in the supply cylinder; and

↘ in the case of airline-fed apparatus (except half-mask respirators used occasionally against dusts or fumes of relatively low toxicity), the flow volume and quality of the supplied air. If the air supply is from a mobile compressor, you should carry out this test immediately before using it for the first time in any new location.

In the case of airline-fed half-mask respirators used occasionally against dusts or fumes of relatively low toxicity, employers and self-employed people will just need to record:

↘ the responsible employer's name and address;

↘ the date of the inspection or test and the name and signature (or unique authentication) of the person who carried it out; and

↘ the condition of the equipment and details of any faults found.

You must make sure it is clear which item of RPE the record relates to.

## 6.8 HEALTH SURVEILLANCE RECORDS

In situations where your employer needs a formal procedure to assess the health of pesticide users, the records should include the following details for every employee using pesticides.

> Their full name, sex, date of birth, permanent address and postcode, National Insurance number, the date their current employment started and a record of any previous jobs where they were exposed to substances health surveillance is needed for.

> The results of all other health surveillance procedures, the dates when they were carried out, and details of who was responsible for each surveillance programme. You should interpret these results in terms of an employee's fitness for their work and include, where appropriate, a record of the medical adviser's or doctor's decisions, or the conclusions of the medical practitioner, occupational health nurse or other suitably qualified or responsible person. You should not include confidential clinical information.

> If health surveillance involves only keeping an individual health record, you should record the details listed in the first bullet point above.

> As well as these detailed records, you should also keep an index or list of the names of people who are undergoing, or have undergone, health surveillance.

Employers should make sure they keep records for the appropriate length of time (see table 7) and that they can be referred to easily. This is particularly important if there are significant changes in the business (such as a change of ownership or change of business activities). In the case of health surveillance records, if a business stops trading, the employer should offer these records to the HSE.

## 6.9 DISPOSAL RECORDS

If you are moving or disposing of waste, you must keep a copy of each 'waste transfer note' (and a written description of the waste) for at least two years. For special waste, you must keep a copy of each 'consignment note' for at least three years.

TABLE 7 Summary of records to be kept

| Type of record | Time kept for | Reason for records |
|---|---|---|
| Pesticide store records | Until updated | To give an accurate list of the contents of your chemical store in an emergency. |
| | | To help you with stock control. |
| Pesticide treatments | To be decided | To show that you have used pesticides appropriately, safely and legally. By law, food producers must keep these records. At present it is good practice for all other professional users to keep records, but this will be law in the future. |
| | | To help with good management. |
| | | To provide other people with important information, especially in emergencies when people, animals or the environment have accidentally been contaminated, or crops have been damaged. |
| | | To help you keep track of periods when crops cannot be harvested and people or animals cannot enter a treated area. |
| | | To meet the specific conditions of crop assurance schemes or the woodland assurance standard. |
| LERAPs | Three years | To show that you have met the conditions of the LERAP schemes. |
| | | To show that you have met the conditions of agri-environment or stewardship schemes. |
| | | To allow you to assess the effectiveness of a particular pesticide. |
| | | To meet the specific conditions of crop assurance schemes or the woodland assurance standard. |

| Type of record | Time kept for | Reason for records |
| --- | --- | --- |
| COSHH assessment and environmental risk assessment | Until revised | To show that you have adequately assessed all risks to people and the environment. |
| | | To provide evidence that you have met your legal obligations to protect people and the environment. |
| | | To confirm that you have the appropriate certificates or permission (for example, authorisations under the Groundwater Regulations). |
| Maintenance, inspection and testing of measures to control exposure | Five years | To confirm that measures to control exposure are working effectively. |
| | | To show that employers have met their legal duty to maintain, inspect and test engineering controls and respiratory protective equipment. |
| Monitoring exposure in the workplace (general samples from the workplace) | Five years | To confirm that the level of exposure at work is acceptable. |
| Monitoring exposure of individual, identifiable people | Forty years | To show that employers have achieved and maintained adequate control of exposure to dangerous substances. |
| Health surveillance | Forty years | To identify any negative health effects resulting from exposure to dangerous substances at work. |
| | | To show that employers have met any legal conditions to carry out health surveillance of their employees. |
| Disposal records | Two or three years (see **section 6.9**) | To show that waste has been handled and disposed of safely and legally. |

# ANNEX A

7

# LAWS REFERRED TO IN THIS CODE

# ANNEX A LAWS REFERRED TO IN THIS CODE

**1** This code reflects the following laws and sets out the best practice to make sure you meet your legal obligations. If the law listed applies only to certain parts of the United Kingdom, there is likely to be a similar law applying elsewhere in the United Kingdom. In general, laws relating to human health and safety are enforced by the Health and Safety Executive, and environmental law is enforced by the Scottish Environment Protection Agency in Scotland.

**2** FOOD AND ENVIRONMENT PROTECTION ACT 1985 (FEPA)

Part III of FEPA aims to:

↘ protect the health of people, creatures and plants;

↘ protect the environment; and

↘ establish safe, effective and humane methods of controlling pests.

This act also sets out arrangements for enforcing its requirements and aims to make information about pesticides available to the public.

Part III of FEPA applies to:

↘ any pesticide; or

↘ any substance, preparation or organism that is prepared or used for the purpose of:

- protecting plants, wood or other plant products from harmful organisms;

- regulating the growth of plants;

- controlling against harmful creatures;

- controlling organisms with harmful or unwanted effects on water systems (including sewage treatment works), buildings or other structures, or on manufactured products; and

- protecting animals against parasites.

**3** CONTROL OF PESTICIDES REGULATIONS 1986 (AS AMENDED) (COPR)

These regulations, made under FEPA, specify that:

⬎ all pesticide products must be approved by Ministers; and

⬎ pesticides can only be sold, supplied, stored, advertised or used in line with the regulations.

Under COPR, anyone who uses pesticides in the course of their work must have received training in using them in a safe, efficient and humane way and have the knowledge, skills and experience needed for the duties they will perform. Also, any person who uses a pesticide must use it only on the land, crop, structure, material or other area being treated.

**4** PLANT PROTECTION PRODUCTS (SCOTLAND) REGULATIONS 2005 (PPPR) AND PLANT PROTECTION PRODUCTS (BASIC CONDITIONS) REGULATIONS 1997

PPPR continues to implement, in Scotland, European Council Directive 91/414/EEC concerning the placing of plant protection products on the market. The Directive aims to make the approval of plant protection products consistent throughout the European Union. The Basic Conditions Regulations define the conditions for selling, supplying, storing, advertising and using pesticides approved under PPPR (and are essentially the same as for pesticide products approved under COPR). These regulations, made under the European Council Directive, apply to new active substances and to older actives once they have been reviewed in the European Union.

**5** HEALTH AND SAFETY AT WORK ETC. ACT 1974 (HSWA)

This act gives people the following obligations:

⬎ Employers must protect (as far as is reasonably possible) the health, safety and welfare of their employees while at work. This includes providing the necessary information, training, supervision and protective equipment to carry out any job safely, and to protect employees and others;

⬎ Employees and the self-employed must take reasonable care of their own health and the safety of others. This includes wearing suitable protective equipment;

⬎ Suppliers must make sure that substances are safe and do not put health at risk when they are being used, handled, stored or transported. Suppliers must provide information about risks and how the substances can be safely used and disposed of.

**6** CONTROL OF SUBSTANCES HAZARDOUS TO HEALTH REGULATIONS 2002 (COSHH)

Under the COSHH regulations there is a legal duty to:

⬎ assess the risks to health when working with substances which are dangerous to people's health (which includes many pesticides); and

⬎ eliminate or, if this is not reasonably possible, adequately control exposure to these substances.

**7** MANAGEMENT OF HEALTH AND SAFETY AT WORK REGULATIONS 1999

These regulations, which bring the European Health and Safety Framework Directive into force in the UK:

⬎ give employers general obligations to improve health and safety management; and

⬎ explain what employers and employees must do under the Health and Safety at Work Act.

## 8 PERSONAL PROTECTIVE EQUIPMENT AT WORK REGULATIONS 1992

These regulations:

- ⬔ set out the principles for choosing, providing, maintaining and using personal protective equipment (PPE); and

- ⬔ order that PPE is suitable for both the person using it and the risks it protects against.

These regulations do not replace specific laws dealing with providing appropriate PPE in certain situations.

## 9 NATURE CONSERVATION (SCOTLAND) ACT 2004 AND THE WILDLIFE AND COUNTRYSIDE ACT 1981 (AS AMENDED)

The Nature Conservation (Scotland) Act 2004 is the principal legislative mechanism which protects wildlife and habitats in Scotland. It replaces the Site of Special Scientific Interest (SSSI) provisions in the Wildlife and Countryside Act 1981 and amends the wildlife protection provisions in Part I of the 1981 Act. The 2004 Act introduces significantly enhanced penalties for intentional or reckless damage to SSSIs, including damage by third parties. Such damage includes acts which cause the protected features on a site to deteriorate. The Act also introduces a specific offence of possessing certain pesticides without lawful excuse. The 2004 Act should be read in conjunction with the Conservation (Natural Habitats &c.) Regulations 1994, which provide specific protection to sites and species of European importance, and Part I of the 1981 Act. Between them these instruments implement the Convention on the Conservation of European Wildlife and Natural Habitats (the 'Bern Convention') and the European Union Directives on the Conservation of Wild Birds (79/409/EEC) and Natural Habitats and Wild Fauna and Flora (92/43/EEC).

## 10 WATER ENVIRONMENT AND WATER SERVICES (SCOTLAND) ACT 2003

The Water Environment and Water Services (Scotland) Act 2003, which transposes the Water Framework Directive (2000) into Scottish law, sets out arrangements for the protection of the water environment. The Act requires the Scottish Executive to introduce controls on all human impacts on the water environment – including point source pollution, pollution from diffuse sources, abstractions and engineering works in the vicinity of the water environment.

## 11 THE WATER ENVIRONMENT (CONTROLLED ACTIVITIES) (SCOTLAND) REGULATIONS 2005 (CAR)

These regulations are made under section 20 of the Water Environment and Water Services (Scotland) Act 2003. CAR will be the major measure in Scotland for achieving the environmental objectives of the Water Framework Directive. The regulations charge the Scottish Environment Protection Agency with authorising activities which pose a risk to the water environment in Scotland, and with striking a balance between environmental protection and the continued sustainable use of the water environment by operators who are dependent on this resource for their economic viability. The activities which will be controlled by the regulations include impoundments, abstractions, engineering in the water environment, discharges and diffuse pollution. CAR has superseded in Scotland the Groundwater Regulations 1998 and similarly provides for the protection of groundwater in line with the Groundwater Directive (80/68/EEC) by controlling the disposal of certain substances, including all pesticides.

**12** FOOD HYGIENE (SCOTLAND) REGULATIONS 2006

These regulations which implement EC Regulation NO 852/2004 on the hygiene of foodstuffs are designed to make sure that there is a high level of protection in food production from the farmer or grower to the consumer ('from farm gate to plate'). The regulations say that risks from food should be identified and controlled and that food and food ingredients should be able to be traced along the food chain to make sure that food is safe.

The regulations came into force on 11 January 2006 and say that people who produce or harvest plant products must keep records of any plant protection products and biocides used.

**13** FEED (HYGIENE AND ENFORCEMENT) (SCOTLAND) REGULATIONS 2005

These regulations which implement EC Regulation NO 183/2005 on the hygiene of feed, are designed to make sure that in the production of animal feed, there is a high level of protection from the farmer or grower to the consumer ('from farm gate to plate'). The regulations say that risks from food should be identified and controlled and that feed and feed ingredients should be able to be traced along the food chain to make sure that all feed and foodstuffs are safe.

The regulations came into force on 1 January 2006 and say that people who produce or harvest plant products for feed to livestock must keep records of any plant protection products and biocides used.

OTHER LAWS

Although not an obligation under FEPA, this code also provides advice on good practice for transporting and disposing of pesticides.

**14** CARRIAGE OF DANGEROUS GOODS AND USE OF TRANSPORTABLE PRESSURE EQUIPMENT REGULATIONS 2004 (AS AMENDED)

These regulations place conditions on those who carry dangerous goods by road or rail (or who use transportable pressure containers). The conditions relate to vehicle design and construction, vehicle markings, transport documents, the type of goods transported, packaging, labelling, training and providing information.

**15** CHEMICALS (HAZARD INFORMATION AND PACKAGING FOR SUPPLY) REGULATIONS 2002 (CHIP)

These regulations set out the conditions for classifying and labelling dangerous substances on the basis of their hazardous properties.

The labelling necessary to reflect the hazard classification includes:

↘ hazard symbols;

↘ standard risk phrases (R-phrases); and

↘ standard safety phrases (S-phrases).

Manufacturers, importers and other suppliers are responsible for classifying and labelling dangerous substances.

**16** CLEAN AIR ACT 1993

This act applies to pollution by smoke, grit and dust from fires and commercial and industrial processes that are not covered by other laws.

7

**17** CONSERVATION OF NATURAL HABITATS AND OF WILD FAUNA AND FLORA 92/43/EEC ('HABITATS DIRECTIVE')

Under this directive, which is how the EC meets its obligations under the Bern Convention, member states must protect natural habitats and important wild species. Member states must:

↘ protect the habitats and species listed in the annexes to the directive;

↘ monitor and report on habitats and species;

↘ propose, prepare and maintain national sites to form a European network of protected sites (Natura 2000 sites); and

↘ control development and other projects which may affect these sites.

**18** CONSERVATION (NATURAL HABITATS, &c.) REGULATIONS 1994 ('HABITATS REGULATIONS')

These regulations bring into force the obligations of the 'Habitats Directive' in Great Britain, setting out the procedure for:

↘ choosing conservation sites;

↘ assessing and reporting on habitats and species in conservation sites; and

↘ assessing and controlling projects affecting Natura 2000 sites.

**19** LAND REFORM (SCOTLAND) ACT 2003

This act establishes the right of responsible access to land and inland water in Scotland for recreation and passage, and places duties in relation to that access.

## 20 ENVIRONMENT ACT 1995

This act created Environment Agencies and introduced arrangements for:

↘ cleaning up contaminated land;

↘ protecting water;

↘ managing air quality; and

↘ reducing packaging waste.

Under this act, the Environment Agencies have powers to give polluters (or potential polluters) notice to carry out work to clean up or prevent pollution. Discharges to controlled waters require a consent from the Scottish Environment Protection Agency. SEPA may carry out anti-pollution work if they think that controlled waters have been (or are likely to be) polluted, and then recover costs from the polluters.

## 21 ENVIRONMENTAL PROTECTION ACT 1990 (AS AMENDED)

Under this act, it is an offence to treat, keep or dispose of 'controlled waste' in a way likely to pollute the environment or harm people. It is also an offence to keep, treat or dispose of 'controlled waste' without a waste-management licence, unless the activity in question is 'exempt' under the Waste Management Licensing Regulations 1994. Under the act, people who produce waste must make sure that it is passed only to an authorised person who can transport, recycle or dispose of it safely.

## 22 ENVIRONMENTAL PROTECTION (DUTY OF CARE) REGULATIONS 1991

These regulations describe the actions which anyone who produces, imports, keeps, stores, transports, treats, recycles or disposes of 'controlled waste' must take. These people must:

- store the waste safely so that it does not cause pollution or harm anyone;

- transfer it only to someone who is authorised to take it (such as someone who holds a waste-management licence or is a registered waste carrier); and

- when passing it on to someone else, provide a written description of the waste and fill in a waste transfer note. These records must be kept for two years and a copy must be provided to the Scottish Environment Protection Agency if they ask for one.

## 23 HAZARDOUS WASTE DIRECTIVE (HWD) (91/689/EEC) AND THE EUROPEAN WASTE CATALOGUE (EWC) (200/532/EC)

This directive aims to provide a precise definition of 'hazardous waste' (known as 'special' waste in Scotland and sets out a framework for correctly managing and regulating the waste. Hazardous waste is any waste on a list drawn up by the European Commission, or waste which has one or more of the hazardous properties set out in the HWD (for example, being explosive, toxic, oxidising, flammable or an irritant).

## 24 HEALTH AND SAFETY (CONSULTATION WITH EMPLOYEES) REGULATIONS 1996 (HSCER)

Under these regulations, any employees not in groups covered by safety representatives from the trade union must be consulted by their employers, either directly or through elected representatives. Elected representatives can:

- talk to employers about concerns on possible risks and dangerous events in the workplace;

- talk to employers about general matters affecting the health and safety of the employees they represent; and

- represent the employees who elected them, in consultation with health and safety inspectors.

## 25 LANDFILL DIRECTIVE (99/31/EC)

This directive aims to prevent or reduce (as far as possible) damage to the environment from disposing of waste to landfill by:

- setting targets for diverting waste away from landfill to other disposal methods (with targets for recovering and recycling waste and reducing the amount of bio-degradable household waste disposed of to landfill);

- pre-treating of waste before it is disposed of to landfill;

- classifying landfill sites as 'hazardous', 'non-hazardous' and 'inert' according to the type of waste they can handle (and banning the disposal of both hazardous and non-hazardous wastes to landfill); and

- banning (or phasing out) the disposal of certain wastes to landfill.

### 26 LANDFILL (SCOTLAND) REGULATIONS 2003

These regulations, which include agricultural waste, make it an offence to landfill (including in a farm dump) or deposit waste for longer than a year without a landfill permit from the Scottish Environment Protection Agency. They fulfil the technical requirements of the Landfill Directive.

### 27 MANUAL HANDLING OPERATIONS REGULATIONS 1992

These regulations make it necessary that, where reasonably possible, pesticides are not handled by people. When lifting, carrying and so on has to be done by hand, a risk assessment must be carried out if there is a risk of injury.

### 28 PROVISION AND USE OF WORK EQUIPMENT REGULATIONS 1998 (PUWER)

Under these regulations, using any mobile work equipment must not result in health and safety problems. Equipment must:

- meet and be maintained to the relevant CE standards;

- be used only for the intended purpose;

- be used only by a trained person; and

- have factory-installed safety features.

### 29 SAFETY REPRESENTATIVES AND SAFETY COMMITTEES REGULATIONS 1977 (SRSCR)

Under these regulations, if an employer recognises a trade union and that trade union has appointed (or is about to appoint) safety representatives, the employer must consult those safety representatives on matters affecting the group (or groups) of employees they represent. Members of these groups of employees may include people who are not members of that trade union. The trade union's safety representatives can:

- investigate and talk to the employer about possible dangers at work, the causes of accidents, and general complaints employees make about health, safety and welfare issues;

- carry out inspections of the workplace;

- represent employees in discussions with health and safety inspectors, and receive information from inspectors; and

- go to meetings of safety committees.

### 30 SPECIAL WASTE REGULATIONS 1996 (AS AMENDED)

These regulations affect people who produce, carry, receive, keep, treat (including recovery) or dispose of waste that is classified as 'special' or hazardous. They were amended during 2004 to include agricultural wastes, and to reflect the most recent Europe-wide list of hazardous wastes. Those parties who deal with special wastes have to obtain consignment notes tracking these wastes from source to recovery or disposal from the Scottish Environment Protection Agency.

7

### 31 WASTE FRAMEWORK DIRECTIVE 75/442/EEC (AMENDED UNDER EC DIRECTIVE 91/156/EEC)

Under these directives, waste must be disposed of without causing danger to people or the environment, and waste management must include plans to reduce, reuse and recycle waste.

### 32 WASTE (SCOTLAND) REGULATIONS 2005

These regulations extend the controlled waste regime in Scotland to all forms of farm waste, and also to non-mineral wastes from mines and quarries.

### 33 WASTE MANAGEMENT LICENSING REGULATIONS 1994 (AS AMENDED)

Under these regulations, people who deposit, recover or dispose of 'controlled waste', or store more than 23,000 litres of 'special waste' must have a waste management licence. The regulations specify which activities qualify for a licensing exemption and cover the use of exempt incinerators. Unless it is carried by the producer, 'controlled waste' must be transported by a waste carrier who is registered with the Scottish Environment Protection Agency, or by an exempt carrier. Licensing exemptions have to be registered with the Scottish Environment Protection Agency.

ANNEXES

# ANNEX B

**THIS IS A LIST OF DIFFERENT BOOKS, LEAFLETS AND LAWS WHICH YOU MAY FIND USEFUL.**

# ANNEX B BIBLIOGRAPHY

**34** ACTS OF WESTMINSTER PARLIAMENT

Clean Air Act 1993, ISBN 010541193

Control of Pollution Act 1974, ISBN 010544074

Environment Act 1995, ISBN 0105425958

Environmental Protection Act 1990, ISBN 0105443905

Food and Environment Protection Act 1985 (FEPA),ISBN 010544885

Health and Safety at Work etc. Act 1974 (HSWA), ISBN 0105437743

Poisons Act 1972, ISBN 0105466727

Water Act 1989, ISBN 010545791

Water Resources Act 1991, ISBN 0105457914

Wildlife and Countryside Act 1981, ISBN 0105469815

**35** ACTS OF SCOTTISH PARLIAMENT

Land Reform (Scotland) Act 2003, ISBN 0105900443

Water Environment and Water Services (Scotland) Act 2003,
ISBN 0105900451

Nature Conservation (Scotland) Act 2004, ISBN 0105900672

**36** REGULATIONS

Carriage of Dangerous Goods and Use of Transportable Pressure Equipment
Regulations 2004, SI 568, ISBN 0110490630

Chemicals (Hazard Information and Packaging for Supply) Regulations 2002
(CHIP), SI 1746, ISBN 0110347463

Conservation (Natural Habitats, &c.) Regulations 1994 ('Habitats
Regulations'), SI 2716, ISBN 0110457161

Control of Pesticides Regulations 1986 (COPR), SI 1510, ISBN 011067510X

Control of Pesticides (Amendment) Regulations 1997, SI 188,
ISBN 0110636953

Control of Substances Hazardous to Health Regulations 2002 (COSHH),
SI 2677, ISBN 0110429192

ANNEXES

Environmental Protection (Duty of Care) Regulations 1991, SI 2389, ISBN 0110158539

Feed (Hygiene and Enforcement) (Scotland) Regulations 2005, SSI 608, ISBN 0110698428

Food Hygiene (Scotland) Regulations 2006, SSI 3, ISBN 0110698983

Groundwater Regulations 1998 (GWR), SI 2746, ISBN 011079799X

Health and Safety (Consultation with Employees) Regulations 1996 (HSCER), SI 1513, ISBN 0110548396

Health and Safety (First Aid) Regulations 1981, SI 917, ISBN 0110169174

Landfill (Scotland) Regulations 2003, SSI 235, ISBN 0110622979

Landfill (Scotland) Amendment Regulations 2003, SSI 343, ISBN 0110624017

Management of Health and Safety at Work Regulations 1999, SI 3242, ISBN 0110250516

Manual Handling Operations Regulations 1992, SI 2793, ISBN 0110259203

Personal Protective Equipment at Work Regulations 1992, SI 3139, ISBN 011025252

Plant Protection Products (Scotland) Regulations 2005, SSI 331, ISBN 0110696158

Plant Protection Products (Basic Conditions) Regulations 1997, SI 189, ISBN 0110696158

Poisons List Order 1982 (as amended), SI 217, ISBN 0110262174

Poisons Rules 1982, SI 218, ISBN 0110262182

Provision and Use of Work Equipment Regulations 1998 (PUWER), SI 2306, ISBN 0110795997

Reporting of Injuries, Diseases and Dangerous Occurrences Regulations 1995 (RIDDOR), SI 3163, ISBN 0110537413

Safety Representatives and Safety Committees Regulations 1977 (SRSCR), SI 500, ISBN 0110705009

Special Waste Regulations 1996, SI 972, ISBN 0110528654

Special Waste Amendment (Scotland) Regulations 2004, SSI 112, ISBN 0110690303

Waste (Scotland) Regulations 2005, SSI 22, ISBN 0110694007

Waste Management Licensing Amendment (Scotland) Regulations 2003, SSI 171, ISBN 0110623010

Waste Management Licensing Regulations 1994, SI 1056, ISBN 0110440560

Water Environment (Controlled Activities) (Scotland) Regulations 2005, SSI 348, ISBN 0110696379

Workplace (Health, Safety and Welfare) Regulations 1992, SI 3004, ISBN 0110258045

## 37 CODES OF PRACTICE

Code of Best Practice: Safe use of sulphuric acid as an agricultural desiccant, National Association of Agricultural Contractors (NAAC), 2002 (also at www.naac.co.uk?Codes/acidcode.asp)

Code of Good Practice for the Prevention of Environmental Pollution From Agricultural Activity (PEPFAA), Scottish Executive ISBN 0755941063

Code of Good Practice for the Prevention of Environmental Pollution From Agricultural Activity:
Dos and Don'ts Guide (PEPFAA Dos and Don'ts), Scottish Executive

Code of Practice to Prevent the Spread of Ragwort, Defra PB9840

Code of Practice for Suppliers of Pesticides to Agriculture, Horticulture and Forestry (the Yellow Code), Defra PB0091

Control of Substances Hazardous to Health 2002 Approved Code of Practice and Guidance, HSE L5, ISBN 0717625346

Horticulture Code of Practice for Scotland – Helping to Prevent the Spread of Invasive Non-native Species, Scottish Executive (also at www.scotland.gov.uk/invasivespecies)

Management of Health and Safety at Work Regulations 1999. Approved Code of Practice and Guidance, HSE L21, ISBN 071762488-9

Safe Use of Pesticides for Non-agricultural Purposes. HSE Approved Code of Practice, HSE L9, 1995, ISBN 0717605426

The Compilation of Safety Data Sheets (Third Edition), HSE L130, 2002, ISBN 0717623718

Waste Management, the Duty of Care, a Code of Practice, Defra, 1996, ISBN 011753210X (also at www.defra.gov.uk/environment/waste/management/doc/pdf/waste_man_duty-code.pdf)

OTHER GOVERNMENT PUBLICATIONS

**38** CIVIL AVIATION AUTHORITY (CAA)

Information on Requirements to be met by Applicants and Holders of the Aerial Application Certificate, CAA CAP 414

**39** DEPARTMENT FOR ENVIRONMENT, FOOD AND RURAL AFFAIRS (DEFRA) AND THE PESTICIDES SAFETY DIRECTORATE (PSD)

Guidelines for the Use of Herbicides on Weeds In or Near Watercourses and Lakes, Defra, PB 2289

Local Environment Risk Assessment for Pesticides (LERAP): Broadcast Air-assisted Sprayers, Defra (also at www.pesticides.gov.uk/uploadedfiles/Web_Assets/PSD/LERAP_Horizontal_boom_sprayers.pdf)

Pesticides and Integrated Farm Management, Defra, PB 9241

Pesticide use – the environmental issues, Defra (Pesticides Forum), PB 8653

**40** DEPARTMENT FOR TRANSPORT (DFT)

Working with ADR: an introduction to the carriage of dangerous goods by road, DfT, ISBN 1904763472 (also at www.dft.gov.uk/stellent/groups/dft_transsec/documents/downloadable/dft_transsec_029427.pdf)

**41** ENVIRONMENT AGENCY (EA)

Best Farming Practices: Profiting from a Good Environment, EA

Use of herbicides in or near water, EA

**42** ENGLISH NATURE

The Herbicide Handbook: Guidance on the use of herbicides on nature conservation sites, English Nature in association with Forum for the Application of Conservation Techniques (FACT), 2003, ISBN 1857167465

**43** FORESTRY COMMISSION

Bevan, D (1987) Forest insects, Forestry Commission Handbook 1, The Stationery Office, London

Davies, RJ (1987), Trees and weeds, Forestry Commission Handbook 2, The Stationery Office, London

Dewar, JA (1993), Oil and chemical spillages, Forestry Authority Technical Development Branch Report 7/93, Forestry Commission Technical Development Branch, Ae Village, Dumfries

Heritage, S (1996), Protecting plants from damage by the large pine weevil and black pine beetle, Forestry Commission Research Information Note 268, Forestry Commission, Edinburgh

Heritage, S (1997), Protecting plants from weevil damage by dipping or spraying before planting using aqueous insecticides, Forestry Commission Research Information Note 270, Forestry Commission, Edinburgh

Heritage, S and Johnson, D (1997), The use of post-planting sprays to improve the protection of plants from damage by *Hylobius abietis*, Forestry Commission Research Information Note 272, Forestry Commission, Edinburgh

Pepper, HW (1996), Grey squirrel damage control with warfarin, Forestry Commission Research Information Note 180, Forestry Commission, Edinburgh

Pratt, JE (1996), *Fomes* stump treatment – an update, Forestry Commission Research Information Note 287, Forestry Commission, Edinburgh

Willoughby, I and Dewar, J (1995), The use of herbicides in the forest, Forestry Commission Field Book 8, The Stationery Office, London

Willoughby, I and Clay, D (1996), Herbicides for farm woodlands and short rotation coppice, Forestry Commission Field Book 14, The Stationery Office, London

7

Willoughby, I and Clay, D (1999), Herbicide update, Forestry Commission Technical Paper 28, Forestry Commission, Edinburgh

Forest and Water Guidelines fourth edition, Forestry Commission, Edinburgh

Reducing pesticide use in forestry, Forestry Commission, Edinburgh

UKWAS (2000), The UK Woodland Assurance Scheme Guide to Certification, Forestry Commission, Edinburgh

44 HEALTH AND SAFETY EXECUTIVE (HSE)

A Guide to RIDDOR 1995, L73, ISBN 0717624315

A Guide to the Health and Safety (Consultation with Employees) Regulations 1996, L95, ISBN 0717612341

Approved Supply List, L129, (updated regularly), ISBN 0717623688

Arboriculture and Forestry Advisory Group (AFAG) leaflets:

-   Application of pesticides by hand-held equipment, AFAG 202

-   Planting, AFAG 103

-   Pre-planting spraying of container-grown seedlings, AFAG 102

A Step by Step Guide to COSHH Assessment, HSG97, 2004, ISBN 0717627853

COSHH – A brief guide to the Regulations, INDG136, 2003

COSHH Essentials, ISBN 0717624218 (also at www.coshh-essentials.org.uk)

COSHH in Forestry, 1991 (also at www.hse.gov.uk)

Fumigation Guidance Note, HSG251, 2005, ISBN 0717629996

Guidance on Storing Pesticides for Farmers and Other Professional Users, Agricultural Information Sheet No.16, 2003 (also at www.hse.gov.uk/pubns/ais16.pdf)

Health Surveillance at Work, HSG61, 1999, ISBN 071761705X

Manual Handling Operations Regulations 1992, Guidance on Regulations, L23, ISBN 0717624153

Medical Aspects of Work Related Exposures to Organophosphates MS17, 2000 (third edition), ISBN 0717617750

Monitoring Strategies for Toxic Substances, HSG173, 1997, ISBN 0717614115

Occupational Exposure Limits, EH 40 (updated periodically)

Personal Protective Equipment at Work. Guidance on Regulations, L25, 1992, ISBN 0717604152

Safe use of all-terrain vehicles (ATVs) in agriculture and forestry, AIS 33, 2004 (also at www.hse.gov.uk/pubns/ais33.pdf)

Safe use of rodenticides on farms and holdings, AIS 31, 1999 (also at www.hse.gov.uk/pubns/misc515.pdf)

Safety representatives and safety committees, L87 (third edition), ISBN 0717612201

Successful Health and Safety Management, HSG 65, ISBN 0717612767

The Carriage of Dangerous Goods Explained, Part 1, Guidance for Consignors of Dangerous Goods by Road and Rail, Classification Packaging and Provision of Information, HSG160, ISBN 0717612554

Plus: Supplement to the Carriage of Dangerous Goods Explained, Part 1, SUPP05, 1999, ISBN 0717612554

The Carriage of Dangerous Goods Explained, Part 2: Guidance for Road Vehicle Operators and Others Involved in the Carriage of Dangerous Goods by Road, HSG161, ISBN 0717612538

Plus: Supplement to the Carriage of Dangerous Goods Explained, Part 2, SUPP06, 1999, ISBN 0717612538

The Idiot's Guide to CHIP INDG 350, 2002, ISBN 0717623335

The Selection, Use and Maintenance of Respiratory Protective Equipment, HSG53, ISBN 0717615375

The Storage of Flammable Liquid in Containers, HSG 51, 1998, ISBN 0717614719

Why do I need a safety data sheet? CHIP 3, INDG353, ISBN 071762367X

## 45 SCOTTISH EXECUTIVE

Is your sprayer fit for work? ISBN 0755906608

Keeping Pesticides Out of Water, ISBN 0755906594

Local Environment Risk Assessment For Pesticides (LERAP) Horizontal Boom Sprayers, ISBN 0755903838

Scottish Biodiversity Strategy, ISBN 0755941209

## 46 SCOTTISH ENVIRONMENT PROTECTION AGENCY

The Water Environment (Controlled Activities) (Scotland) Regulations 2005 – A Practical Guide

Controlled Activities Regulations – Guidance for operators of abstractions and impoundments (also at www.sepa.org.uk/publications/wfd/index.htm)

## 47 SCOTTISH NATURAL HERITAGE

The Scottish Outdoor Access Code 2004 (also at www.outdooraccess-scotland.com/default.asp)

The TIBRE Arable Handbook (Targeted Inputs for a Better Rural Environment) www.snh.org.uk/publications/on-line/heritagemanagement/tibre

7

OTHER USEFUL PUBLICATIONS

**48** BASIS (REGISTRATION) LIMITED

Carriage of Dangerous Goods by Road, BASIS

The Carriage of Agrochemicals by Road: Guidance for the Agrochemicals Industry, BASIS

**49** BCPC (FORMERLY THE BRITISH CROP PROTECTION COUNCIL)

Boom and Fruit Sprayer's Handbook, BCPC, 2001, ISBN 1901396029

Hand-Held and Amenity Sprayer's Handbook, BCPC, 2001, ISBN 1901396037.

Safety Equipment Handbook, BCPC, 2002, ISBN 1901396061

The UK Pesticide Guide, BCPC (published every year), 2006, ISBN 0851997376

Using Pesticides – a Complete Guide to Safe, Effective Spraying, BCPC, 1998, ISBN 1901396010

**50** CROP PROTECTION ASSOCIATION (CPA) AND THE VOLUNTARY INITIATIVE (VI)

CPA Best Practice Guides (emergency procedures, avoiding drift, pesticide storage, pesticides and conservation, hand protection, protective equipment, sprayer cleaning, container cleaning, agrochemical disposal, record keeping, pesticide legislation), CPA (also on the Voluntary Initiative website at www. voluntaryinitiative.org.uk/Content/Agr_BP.asp)

Every drop counts: keeping water clean, CPA (also at www.cropprotection.org.uk)

**51** NATIONAL FARMERS UNION (NFU)

Farm Transport of Dangerous Goods, NFU

**52** UNIVERSITY OF HERTFORDSHIRE

Environmental Management for Agriculture (EMA) (see www.herts.ac.uk/aeru/ema/welcome.htm)

ANNEXES

# ANNEX C

124 : PESTICIDES

7

THIS GLOSSARY DEFINES WORDS USED
IN THIS CODE AND OF APPLICATION
EQUIPMENT AND METHODS

# ANNEX C GLOSSARY OF TERMS USED IN THIS CODE AND OF APPLICATION EQUIPMENT AND METHODS

The definitions in this glossary are for guidance only. They are not legally binding, unless it specifically states that the definition is that set by law.

## GLOSSARY 1

This glossary defines words used in this code.

| | |
|---|---|
| Active ingredient | The part of a pesticide product which gives it its pesticidal properties. 'Active substance' is often used to mean the same thing. |
| Active substance | Any substance or micro-organism (including a virus) that has a general or specific action against harmful organisms or on plants, parts of plants or plant products. 'Active ingredient' is often used to mean the same thing. |
| Adjuvant | A substance (other than water) without significant pesticidal properties and which, when added to a pesticide before it is applied, improves or is intended to improve the effectiveness of the pesticide. |
| Aerial application | Applying a pesticide from an aircraft (either fixed-wing or helicopter) in flight. |
| Agricultural vehicle | Any agricultural or forestry tractor or agricultural machinery. |
| Anti-cholinesterase compounds | A class of chemicals that includes many insecticides, such as parathion or carbaryl. They prevent the action of cholinesterase, which can in turn lead to a variety of symptoms such as nausea, vomiting, blurred vision, stomach cramps, and rapid heart rate. |
| Approval | All pesticide products must be approved before they can be advertised, stored, sold, supplied or used. The company wanting to sell a pesticide will usually apply for the approval. It will only be given when all the necessary evidence and information on the safety, effectiveness and, where relevant, the humaneness of the pesticide have been evaluated and considered acceptable. You can find full details of the approvals process on the PSD website (www.pesticides.gov.uk) |

# GLOSSARY OF TERMS USED IN THIS CODE AND OF APPLICATION EQUIPMENT AND METHODS

| | |
|---|---|
| Biobed (lined biobed) | A lined pit, 1 to 1.3 metres deep, filled with a mixture of straw, soil and peat-free compost and then turfed over. When correctly used, biobeds are effective at locking in and breaking down pesticide residues resulting from drips and splashes. In certain circumstances, a lined biobed may also be used to dispose of dilute pesticide from tank washings. |
| Biodiversity (or biological diversity) | The richness, abundance and variety of plant and wildlife species. Both the number of species and the number of individuals within each species are important in considering the biodiversity in an area. |
| Biological agents | Bacteria, viruses, fungi, other micro-organisms and their associated toxins. They can affect human health in a variety of ways, ranging from relatively mild, allergic reactions to serious medical conditions, even death. They are everywhere in the natural environment - in water, soil, plants, and animals. Because many microbes reproduce quickly and need very little to survive, they are a potential danger in a wide variety of occupational settings. |
| Biological monitoring | Measuring and assessing levels of chemicals or their 'metabolites' (substances the body converts the chemical into) in the breath, urine or blood of exposed workers. This monitoring may investigate either the level of exposure to an active substance or look for chemical signs of a reaction to exposure. |
| Bystander | Any person who is in or near the area where a pesticide is being or has been used but is not directly involved in using the pesticide. |
| Catchment | The area of land which water flows from (by run-off, movement through the soil or drainage) to surface water or groundwater. |
| Cholinesterase | An enzyme found primarily at nerve endings. It is important in sending nerve impulses in the body. |
| Closed-transfer system | A way of transferring the necessary amount of a pesticide from its container to the equipment applying it in a closed system to avoid the need for pouring and measuring and so reducing the risk of contamination. Some systems are designed for use with returnable containers. |

7

| | |
|---|---|
| Commodity substance | Substances with an approved pesticidal use which also have other non-pesticidal uses. Approval is given only for using the substance, not for selling, supplying, storing or advertising it. There is no approval holder or approved pesticide product label. You must read, understand and follow the approved conditions of use in the approval. You can look at the approval on the PSD website (www.pesticides.gov.uk). |
| Consent | The detailed rules under Part III of the Food and Environment Protection Act 1985 are set out in what are known as 'consents' to be found in the Schedules to the Control of Pesticides (Amendment) Regulations 1997 and the Plant Protection Products (Basic Conditions) Regulations 1997. These consents are issued by Ministers and permit pesticides to be advertised, sold, stored, supplied and used, subject to certain conditions. These conditions set out general conditions for all pesticide users.

The term 'consent' is also used to describe the regulatory regime in place under the Control of Pollution Act 1974. It is the main legislative vehicle for point source pollution control, and provides a system whereby discharges of pollutants are subject to consent by SEPA. |
| Cross compliance | Standards and requirements which farmers and crofters have to meet as a condition of receiving their Single Farm Payment. These requirements and measures concern the promotion of a more environment-friendly and sustainable approach to farming in Scotland. |
| Following crop | The next crop grown in the treated area, including when it is a treated perennial. |
| Groundwater | All water which is below the surface of the ground in the saturation zone (the soil lying immediately under the top layer of soil) and in direct contact with the ground or subsoil. |
| Landfill site | Defined in the Landfill (Scotland) Regulations 2003 as 'a waste disposal site for the deposit of the waste onto or into land'. This applies to both landfill sites receiving waste from a range of external sources and also internal waste disposal sites used by producers to dispose of waste at the site where it is produced. |

ANNEXES

# GLOSSARY OF TERMS USED IN THIS CODE AND OF APPLICATION EQUIPMENT AND METHODS

| | |
|---|---|
| Leaching | The movement of pesticide residues through the soil by water filtering through the ground. |
| Local Environment Risk Assessment for Pesticides (LERAP) | For certain pesticides you must leave 'buffer zones' (untreated areas) to protect water and anything living in it when you are applying pesticide with a ground crop sprayer or a broadcast air-assisted sprayer. In some circumstances, the size of the buffer zone needed, as stated on the product label, can be adjusted to suit individual situations by carrying out a LERAP. Details of the LERAP schemes for ground crop sprayers and broadcast air-assisted sprayers are on the PSD website (www.pesticides.gov.uk). |
| Maximum exposure limit (MEL) | The maximum concentration of a substance in the air, averaged over a set period, which people at work can be exposed to under any circumstances. The MEL for each substance that has one is given in Schedule 1 of the COSHH Regulations. These are now referred to as Workplace Exposure Limits. |
| Mixer or loader | A person who is involved in mixing or loading pesticides into the tank or hopper of any application equipment. |
| Occupational exposure standard (OES) | The concentration of a substance in the air, averaged over a set period, at which, according to current knowledge, there is no evidence that it is likely to harm a person at work who repeatedly breathes in that concentration. These are now referred to as Workplace Exposure Limits. |
| Parallel import | An imported pesticide which is identical to a product already approved in the UK. A parallel import also has to get a UK approval before it can be sold, supplied, stored, used or advertised. |
| Personal protective equipment (PPE) | Any device or appliance, which meets the appropriate standards, designed to be worn or held by a person to protect them from one or more health and safety risks. |
| Pesticide | Any substance, preparation or organism that is prepared or used for controlling any pest. |
| Pest | Any organism that is harmful to plants, wood or other plant products, any unwanted plant, or any harmful creature. |

7

| | |
|---|---|
| Pesticide approved for agricultural use | A pesticide (other than one with methyl bromide or chloropicrin as one of its active ingredients) approved for use: |

↘ in agriculture and horticulture (including amenity areas);

↘ in forestry;

↘ in or near water (other than by householders); or

↘ as an industrial herbicide (such as weedkillers for use on land that is not intended for producing any crops).

| | |
|---|---|
| Plant protection product | An active substance or preparation that contains one or more active substances (in the form in which it is supplied to the user) which is intended to: |

↘ protect plants or plant products against all harmful organisms or prevent the action of those organisms;

↘ influence the life processes of plants other than as a nutrient (for example, as a growth regulator);

↘ preserve plant products (except for substances or products which are controlled under European Union law on preservatives);

↘ destroy unwanted plants; or

↘ destroy parts of plants or control or prevent the undesired growth of plants.

| | |
|---|---|
| Reduced-volume spraying | Applying a pesticide in a lower volume of water than the minimum volume recommended on the label for that dose. |
| Respiratory protective equipment (RPE) | Any respiratory or breathing apparatus, which meets the appropriate standards and is designed to prevent or control contamination from breathing in a substance. |
| Special waste | Any waste which is hazardous waste as defined by Article 1(4) of the Hazardous Waste Directive (91/689/EEC). |

Specific off-label approval (SOLA)

Other approved uses of a pesticide product (possibly on a minor crop or in an uncommon situation) as well as the uses described on the product label. If you use a pesticide under a SOLA you must read, understand and follow the approved conditions of use set out in the Notice of Approval for that SOLA. You can view the approval on the PSD website (www.pesticides.gov.uk).

Spray quality

A classification reflecting the size of droplet in a spray, normally expressed in terms of the 'Volume median diameter (VMD)'. Under the British Crop Protection Council (BCPC) scheme, the following categories are used:

| Volume median diameter | Size classification |
|---|---|
| Less than 25$\mu$m | Fine aerosol ('Fog' or 'Very fine spray') |
| 26 to 50$\mu$m | Coarse aerosol ('Fog' or 'Very fine spray') |
| 51 to 100$\mu$m | Mist ('Very fine spray') |
| 101 to 200$\mu$m | Fine spray |
| 201 to 300$\mu$m | Medium spray |
| More than 300$\mu$m | Coarse spray |

| | |
|---|---|
| Substance hazardous to health | Any substance (including any preparation) which: |
| | ↘ is listed in Part I of the Approved Supply List as dangerous within the meaning of the Chemical (Hazard Information and Packaging) Regulations 1993, and which is classified as 'very toxic', 'toxic', 'harmful', 'corrosive' or 'irritant'; |
| | ↘ has a maximum exposure limit specified in Schedule 1 of the COSHH regulations or the Health and Safety Commission has approved an 'occupation exposure standard' for; |
| | ↘ is a biological agent; |
| | ↘ is a dust of any kind when present at a substantial concentration in the air; or |
| | ↘ not mentioned in the list above, but which creates a similar danger to the health of any person. |
| Swale | A broad shallow drain used as part of sustainable urban drainage schemes (SUDS). |
| Tank mix | A spray solution, prepared by the user, containing a mixture of two or more pesticide products. |
| User | Person or persons who use pesticides professionally in the course of their job or business: on farms and holdings; in horticulture; on amenity areas, industrial areas and sports grounds; and in forestry. |
| Water abstraction | Removing water, either permanently or temporarily, from any source including groundwater (for example, wells and boreholes) or surface water (rivers, streams, lakes and coastal waters). In the UK, the main water abstractors are statutory water supply undertakers, households, irrigated agriculture, industry and energy generators. |
| Workplace exposure limit (WEL) | New terminology for Maximum Exposure Limit (MEL), see entry under MEL. |

## GLOSSARY 2

The definitions in glossary 2 relate to equipment and methods of applying pesticides. They are loosely based on the NPTC assessment schedules for certificates of competence in using pesticides safely.

| | |
|---|---|
| Air assistance | Using forced air to carry spray droplets to their intended target (see '**Broadcast air-assisted spraying**' and '**Downward placement air-assisted spraying**'). |
| Air-inclusion (air-induction) nozzle | A type of hydraulic nozzle with an air inlet so that the flow of liquid through the nozzle sucks in air which mixes with the spray liquid. These nozzles usually produce a coarse spray with many droplets containing one or more bubbles of air. |
| Broadcast air-assisted spraying | Using any equipment which broadcasts spray droplets, in an air stream produced by forced air, which carry upwards and outwards from the source of the spray. |
| Controlled droplet application (CDA) | CDA means producing only the optimum sizes of spray droplet for the particular application. This is achieved by using a rotary atomiser. See also entry for '**Rotary atomiser**'. |
| Deflector (flooding, anvil, impact) nozzle | A nozzle of either the 'hydraulic' or 'twin-fluid' type which produces a fan-shaped spray pattern when a cylindrical jet of liquid passes through a relatively large hole and hits a smooth, angled surface at a high speed. Generally, for hydraulic types, these nozzles produce relatively large droplets and are used at low pressures. |
| Downward placement air-assisted spraying | Using a forced stream of air to force the pesticide downwards (for example to help it to penetrate a crop canopy or reduce off-target drift). |
| Electrostatically charged | Material which has had an electrostatic charge added to help deposit the pesticide on target. |

7

| | |
|---|---|
| Fog | A space treatment using a droplet with a volume median diameter of less than 50$\mu$m, and with more than 10% of the spray volume having a droplet diameter smaller than 30$\mu$m. This includes both thermal fogs produced in a very hot air flow and cold fogs produced by a whirling mass of air. |
| Fumigation | An operation in which the pesticide acts as a gas, although it may not be applied in the form of a gas, to control or kill pests or other undesirable organisms. |
| Granule applicator | Any equipment, possibly air-assisted, which applies pesticides in granule form. |
| Ground crop sprayer | Any equipment of the spray boom type which applies pesticides using a horizontal boom. |
| Hand-held applicator | Any equipment carried by a person or where the pesticide delivery nozzle or outlet is supported directly by the user. |
| Hydraulic nozzle | A device though which spray liquid is given out, broken up into droplets and scattered using the pressurised liquid as the energy source. |
| Induction bowl or hopper | Metal, plastic or fibreglass hoppers attached to the side of the sprayer or the nurse tank that allow pesticides to be added to the mix tank without the person climbing onto the spray rig. Pesticides are poured into the bowl and water is added to flush out the bowl and carry the pesticide to the spray tank. A rinse nozzle is often mounted inside the bowl for rinsing out empty pesticide containers. |
| Mist | A space treatment using a droplet with a volume median diameter of 51 to 100$\mu$m, and with less than 10% of the volume of the spray having a droplet diameter smaller than 30$\mu$m. |

# THE DEFINITIONS IN GLOSSARY 2 RELATE TO EQUIPMENT AND METHODS OF APPLYING PESTICIDES.

| | |
|---|---|
| Mounted equipment | Any pesticide application equipment which is mounted on, attached to or which forms a permanent part of the prime mover. |
| Pedestrian-controlled equipment | Any equipment which is supported by a mechanical carriage controlled by a person who does not ride in or on the carriage. |
| Pre-orifice nozzle | A hydraulic nozzle which incorporates a second hole upstream of the outlet. This decreases the pressure through the nozzle and so reduces the proportion of small droplets. |
| Prime mover | Any self-propelled vehicle used by a person who rides in or on the vehicle. |
| Roller table equipment (conveyor-belt mounted equipment, planter-mounted equipment and so on) | Application equipment which is mounted on, attached to, or forms a permanent part of a treatment system. |
| Rotary atomiser | A device in which a rotating solid surface, such as a cup, disc, wheel or cage, is the main source of energy used to produce a spray. |
| Seed-treating equipment | Any equipment, either mobile or static, which applies pesticides on cereal grains, pulses and other small seeds. |
| Shrouded boom sprayer | A horizontal boom sprayer, that is mounted on a vehicle, trailed or pedestrian-controlled, and which incorporates a shroud designed to prevent, or reduce, off-target drift. The shroud could be with a flexible skirt in contact with the target. |
| Smoke | A space treatment using a device to produce smoke containing the pesticide's active substance. |
| Spray train | Any vehicle running on rails that has equipment for applying pesticides to the track, trackside or nearby areas and which is mounted on or attached to the vehicle or forms a permanent part of the vehicle. |

| | |
|---|---|
| Sprayer | Any equipment used to apply sprays that have droplets within limits described by the British Crop Protection Council (BCPC nozzle classification scheme as 'coarse', 'medium', 'fine' and 'very fine'. |
| Sub-surface liquid applicator | Any equipment, except pedestrian-controlled equipment, which is designed to apply liquid pesticides below the surface of the ground. |
| Trailed equipment | Any application equipment which is trailed behind the prime mover. |
| Twin-fluid nozzle | A nozzle in which air under pressure is mixed with the spray liquid before it reaches the nozzle's hole. |
| Variable geometry sprayer | Any equipment which applies pesticides using a boom which can be positioned horizontally or vertically to suit the target. |
| Vehicle-mounted kerb sprayer | Any equipment which is mounted on, fixed to, or forms part of any vehicle for applying pesticides on roadside kerbs. |
| Water volume (application volume) | The volume of a spray liquid, including all pesticides, diluents, adjuvants, carriers and other components of the spray solution, applied in each unit area, normally expressed as litres per hectare. |
| Wick applicator or weed wiper | Any equipment which applies pesticides to the target by direct contact with an impregnated absorbent surface (wick, pad or roller). |

# ANNEX D

## ADDRESSES

# ANNEX D ADDRESSES

**ADAS Scotland**
Royal Highland Centre
Ingliston
Edinburgh
EH28 8NF
Phone: 0131 335 0326
Website: www.adas.co.uk

**Agricultural Engineers Association (AEA)**
Samuelson House
Paxton Road
Orton Centre
Peterborough
Cambridgeshire
PE2 5LT
Phone: 01733 362925
Website: www.aea.uk.com

**Agricultural Industries Confederation (AIC)**
Confederation House
East of England Showground
Peterborough
Cambridgeshire
PE2 6XE
Phone: 01733 385230
Website: www.agindustries.org.uk

**Association of Independent Crop Consultants**
Agriculture House
Station Road
Liss
Hampshire
GU33 7AR
Phone: 023 80895354
Website: www.aicc.org.uk

**BASIS (Registration) Limited**
34 St John Street
Ashbourne
Derbyshire
DE6 1GH
Phone: 01335 343945
Website: www.basis-reg.com

**BCPC (formerly the British Crop Protection Council)**
7 Omni Business Centre
Omega Park
Alton
Hampshire
GU34 2QD
Phone: 01420 593200
Website: www.bcpc.org

ANNEXES

**British Beekeepers' Association**
National Agricultural Centre
Stoneleigh
Kenilworth
Warwickshire
CV8 2LG
Phone: 024 76696679
Website: www.bbka.org.uk

**British Pest Control Association (BPCA)**
1 Gleneagles House
Vernon Gate
South Street
Derby
Derbyshire
DE1 1UP
Phone: 01332 294288
Website: www.bpca.org.uk

**Centre for Aquatic Plant Management (CAPM)**
CEH Wallingford
Maclean Building
Benson Lane
Crowmarsh Gifford
Wallingford
Oxfordshire
OX10 8BB
Phone: 01419 838800
Website: www.capm.org.uk

**Chartered Institution of Wastes Management (CIWM)**
9 Saxon Court
St Peter's Gardens
Marefair
Northampton
NN1 1SX
Phone: 01604 620426
Website: www.ciwm.co.uk

**Crop Protection Association (UK) Limited (CPA)**
4 Lincoln Court
Lincoln Road
Peterborough
Cambridgeshire
PE1 2RP
Phone: 01733 294222
Website: www.cropprotection.org.uk and
www.voluntaryinitiative.org.uk

**Department for Environment, Food and Rural Affairs (Defra)**
Nobel House
17 Smith Square
London
SW1P 3JR
Phone: 020 72386000
Website: www.defra.gov.uk

7

**Farming and Wildlife Advisory Group (FWAG) Scotland**
Algo Business Centre
Glenearn Road
Perth
PH2 0NJ
Phone: 01738 450450
Website: www.fwag.org.uk/scotland

**Forestry Commission**
231 Corstorphine Road
Edinburgh
EH12 7AT
Phone: 0131 334 0303
Website: www.forestry.gov.uk

**The Game Conservancy Trust**
Burgate Manor
Fordingbridge
Hampshire
SP6 1EF
Phone: 01425 652381
Website: www.gct.org.uk

**Health and Safety Executive (HSE)**
HSE Information Services
Caerphilly Business Park
Caerphilly
CF83 3GG
Phone: 0845 3450055
Website: www.hse.gov.uk

Contact your nearest HSE office to report pesticide-related human health incidents. For out-of-hours emergencies,
phone 0151 9229235.

Details of your local HSE office are on the HSE website or see local telephone directory.

**Lantra Sector Skills Council**
Newlands
Scone
Perth
PH2 6NL
Phone: 01738 553311
Website: www.lantra.co.uk/scotland

**Linking Environment and Farming (LEAF)**
National Agricultural Centre
Stoneleigh
Kenilworth
Warwickshire
CV8 2LZ
Phone: 024 76413911
Website: www.leafuk.org

ANNEXES

**National Association of Agricultural Contractors (NAAC)**
Samuelson House
Paxton Road
Orton Centre
Peterborough
Cambridgeshire
PE2 5LT
Phone: 01733 362920
Website: www.naac.co.uk

**National Farmers' Union Scotland**
Head Office
Rural Centre
West Mains
Ingliston
Midlothian
Phone: 0131 472 4000
Website: www.nfus.org.uk

**National Poisons Information Service**
Royal Infirmary of Edinburgh
Little France Crescent
Edinburgh
EH16 4SA
Phone: 0131 242 1381
Website: www.spib.scot.nhs.uk

**National Register of Sprayer Operators (NRoSO)**
NPTC
National Agricultural Centre
Stoneleigh
Warwickshire
CV8 2LG
Phone: 024 76857300
Website: www.nroso.org.uk

**NPTC (formerly National Proficiency Tests Council)**
National Agricultural Centre
Stoneleigh
Kenilworth
Warwickshire
CV8 2LG
Phone: 024 7685 7300
Website: www.nptc.org.uk

**Office of Public Sector Information**
Website: www.opsi.gov.uk
Does not give legal or public sector advice nor sell legislation. You can look legislation up on this site.

**Pesticides Action Network UK (PAN UK)**
Development House
56-64 Leonard Street
London
EC2A 4JX
Phone: 020 70650905
Website: www.pan-uk.org

**Pesticides Safety Directorate (PSD)**
Information Services Branch
Mallard House
Kings Pool
3 Peasholme Green
York
YO1 2PX
Phone: 01904 455775
Website: www.pesticides.gov.uk

**RSPB Scotland**
Dunedin House
25 Ravelston Terrace
Edinburgh
EH4 3TP
Phone: 0131 311 6500
Website: www.rspb.org.uk

**Scottish Agricultural College (SAC)**
SAC Central Office
West Mains Road
Edinburgh
EH9 3JG
Phone: 0131 535 4004
Website: www.sac.ac.uk

**Scottish Beekeepers' Association**
Website: www.scottishbeekeepers.org.uk

**Scottish Biodiversity Forum**
c/o Scottish Executive
Area 1J, Victoria Quay
Leith
Edinburgh
EH6 6QQ
Phone: 0131 244 6328
Website: www.scotland.gov.uk/biodiversity

**Scottish Environment Protection Agency (SEPA)**
Contact your local SEPA office, details of which are on
the SEPA website: www.sepa.org.uk
24-hour emergency telephone: 0800 807060

**Scottish Executive Environment and Rural Affairs
Department (SEERAD)**
Contact your local SEERAD area office
Phone: see local telephone directory
Website: www.scotland.gov.uk

**Scottish Natural Heritage (SNH)**
Great Glen House House
Leachkin Road
Inverness
IV3 8NW
Phone: 01463 725 000
Website: www.snh.org.uk

**Scottish Skills Testing Service**
Ingliston
Edinburgh
EH28 8NE
Phone: 0131 333 2040
Website: www.ssts.co.uk

**Scottish Water**
PO Box 8855
Edinburgh
EH10 6YQ
Phone: Business Customer Helpline: 0845 602 8855
Emergency Helpline: 0845 600 8855
Website: www.scottishwater.co.uk

**Stationery Office**
TSO Scotland Bookshop
71 Lothian Road
Edinburgh
EH3 9AZ
Phone: 0870 606 5566
Website: www.tso.co.uk

ANNEXES

# ANNEX E

# GUIDANCE ON USING PERSONAL PROTECTIVE EQUIPMENT

# FOLLOW THE GUIDANCE IN THIS ANNEX WHEN YOU ARE USING A PESTICIDE IN A SITUATION NOT COVERED BY THE PRODUCT LABEL.

## ANNEX E GUIDANCE ON USING PERSONAL PROTECTIVE EQUIPMENT

Follow the guidance in this annex when you are using a pesticide in a situation not covered by the product label (or the appropriate notice of approval when using a pesticide for an approved use not specified on the product label or using a substance that has a non-pesticidal use but is approved for use as a pesticide) or when you need extra protection.

| Situation (some situations occur in more than one row) | Reason | Wear (See the notes at the end of this table for details) |
|---|---|---|
| ⬂ All situations (including all those set out below) | Good occupational hygiene practice, to avoid exposure of your hands and skin and to keep your personal clothing clean | Coverall<br><br>Gloves<br><br>Boots |
| ⬂ Preparing products<br><br>⬂ Handling contaminated equipment and containers | To avoid exposure to 'very toxic', 'toxic' or 'corrosive' products | Apron (for liquid products), coveralls, gloves and boots |
| ⬂ Handling and applying dusts<br><br>⬂ Handling contaminated equipment and empty containers after applying dusts<br><br>⬂ Handling and applying 'very toxic' granules<br><br>⬂ Applying fogs, smoke or gases<br><br>⬂ Handling liquid products<br><br>⬂ Applying to targets above waist height<br><br>⬂ Applying indoors (for example, to protected crops)<br><br>⬂ Cleaning equipment used to apply pesticide | To avoid the chance of eye, face or head contamination (for example, by splashes or contact with droplets or particles in the air) | Face-shield for splashes, hood, coveralls, gloves and boots |

| Situation (some situations occur in more than one row) | Reason | Wear (See the notes at the end of this table for details) |
|---|---|---|
| ↘ Handling and applying dusts<br><br>↘ Handling contaminated equipment and empty containers after applying dusts<br><br>↘ Handling and applying 'very toxic' granules<br><br>↘ Applying fogs, smokes or gases | To avoid breathing in droplets, particles or gases in the air | Respiratory protective equipment (full-face type if product is 'very toxic'), coveralls, gloves and boots |
| ↘ Reduced-volume spraying outdoors by a vehicle without a closed cab or hand-held sprayers | To avoid increased exposure from using a more concentrated spray solution | Face-shield, coveralls, gloves and boots<br><br>Hood for 'harmful' or 'irritant' products and coveralls, gloves and boots |
| ↘ Reduced-volume spraying by indoor sprayers and outdoor equipment on a vehicle without a closed cab | To avoid increased exposure from using a more concentrated spray solution | Face-shield, RPE, hood, an apron for 'harmful' or 'irritant' products, and coveralls, gloves and boots |
| ↘ Applications using ATV-mounted or trailed equipment<br><br>↘ Applying from tractors without closed cabs | To avoid increased exposure from using a vehicle without a closed cab | Face-shield, hood, coveralls, gloves and boots |

**Coveralls** – choose your coveralls for the particular purpose, in line with the following table.

| Purpose | CEN type | Description |
| --- | --- | --- |
| Protection against:<br><br>liquid jets | Type 3 | Chemical protective clothing where liquid cannot pass through the connections between different parts of the clothing |
| sprays | Type 4 | Chemical protective clothing where spray cannot pass through the connections between different parts of the clothing |
| solid particles | Type 5 | Reusable and limited-use protective clothing which particles cannot pass through |
| liquid splashes and solid particles | Type 6 | Reusable and limited-use protective clothing offering limited protection against liquid splashes and aerosols and solid particles |

**Gloves** – unless the pesticide label or a specific COSHH assessment says otherwise, gloves should be made from nitrile rubber, be at least 0.5 millimetres thick and at least 300 millimetres long. Gloves should be taken off when entering 'clean' areas such as tractor cabs.

**Boots** – appropriate boots are wellington boots or waterproof footwear

**Face-shields** – choose face-shields that give full protection of your face and do not mist up when you use them (anti-mist visors).

**Respiratory protective equipment** – your choice will depend on the product label and a COSHH assessment. Consider the following as the basic conditions.

| | |
| --- | --- |
| Potential dust particles or spray droplets in the air | Use an EN 149 particle-filtering half mask FF2-SL or EN 140 + 143 half mask connected to particle filter P2 |
| Potential vapour in the air | Use an EN 140 + 141 half mask connected to combined filters A1P2 |

**Open-backed cabs** – open cabs (including cabs with open rear windows) do not count as closed cabs as spray can be drawn inside.

ANNEXES

# ANNEX F

## RECORD SHEET FOR
## PESTICIDE TREATMENTS

# ANNEX F RECORD SHEET FOR PESTICIDE TREATMENTS

You might find this record of your pesticide treatments useful. You may want to add or take away columns because of the specific circumstances of your particular treatments. If you are keeping written records rather than computer ones, you might want to use a large book opened to a double page to give yourself plenty of room to add or take away columns, record different information and so on. You will then be able to see all of the information at once.

The notes referred to in the columns are at the bottom.

| Worker's name | Job reference | Date | Site treated | Crop, area, material or structure treated | Reason for treatment | Product and MAPP or HSE number (see note 1) | Dose of product applied (litres or kilograms per hectare) |
|---|---|---|---|---|---|---|---|
|  |  |  |  |  |  |  |  |
|  |  |  |  |  |  |  |  |

**Note 1:** show all products when a mixture is used.

**Note 2:** you should record:

⬐ periods when crops should not be harvested, people or animals should not be allowed on the site, or ventilation is needed, as appropriate;

⬐ whether the crop or weeds are in flower;

⬐ whether you have told neighbours, beekeepers or others;

⬐ whether you have displayed (and removed) warning signs; and

⬐ whether you had any problems when using the pesticide.

| Volume applied (litres per hectare) | Total amount of product used (litres or kilograms) | Total area treated (hectares or square metres) | Start time | Finish time | Total hours | Weather conditions (such as wind speed and direction) | Other relevant information (see note 2) |
|---|---|---|---|---|---|---|---|
|  |  |  |  |  |  |  |  |
|  |  |  |  |  |  |  |  |

It is good practice to make a note of the effectiveness of the treatment and any damage noticed after an appropriate time.

You may need to make extra records, where appropriate. For example:

⬐ to meet the conditions of the LERAP schemes, crop assurance schemes or the woodland assurance standard; or

⬐ when you are applying certain pesticides or working in certain situations (see **section 4** of this code).

# ANNEX G

# APPLYING PESTICIDES FROM
# AN AIRCRAFT

# ANNEX G APPLYING PESTICIDES FROM AN AIRCRAFT

**53** You must meet specific legal obligations before, during and after applying pesticide from the air. You can only use products which are specifically approved for this purpose, and you must regularly send details of all pesticide applied from aircraft to:

> Pesticides Usage Survey Group (PUSG)
> Defra
> Central Science Laboratory
> Sand Hutton Lane
> Sand Hutton
> York.
> YO41 1LZ

You must follow the conditions of use shown on the product label when applying pesticides from the air.

Everyone applying pesticides from an aircraft must hold a Civil Aviation Authority qualification (the aerial application certificate) and, in the case of contractors or people born after 31 December 1964, the appropriate certificate of competence in applying pesticides.

Under the Control of Pesticides Regulations 1986 (as amended) you must give notice to specific organisations before applying a pesticide from the air. You will also need to consult the following organisations (see below) and get their agreement before carrying out the treatment.

Note:- The Scottish Environment Protection Agency has developed a multi-agency form, which is intended to be used to submit details to SEPA, local authorities and Scottish Natural Heritage.

## 54 CONSULTATION

Consultation means more than just giving notice to the relevant authorities. It should take place well before you intend to apply pesticide and certainly not after the minimum consultation period set by law. The person applying the pesticide will need to provide the information so the organisations consulted can comment in full. You will need to take account of the organisations' views when deciding how to apply the pesticide (or whether to apply it at all). If you are not sure what to do, talk to the organisations concerned for more advice.

Ideally, you will consult the relevant authorities when deciding to use a contractor to apply pesticides from the air. This will give the organisations consulted as much time as possible to consider the matter. They will then have reached a decision by the time you carry out the consultation you need to do by law.

When you give notice that you intend to apply a pesticide from the air, you must include the following information:

↘ The name, address and, where possible, phone number of the person applying the pesticide;

↘ The name of the pesticides you will use and their active ingredients;

↘ The date and time you intend to apply the pesticide;

↘ Confirmation that you have given the same details to your local authority's Environmental Health Department.

**55** CONSULTATION AND CONDITIONS FOR GIVING NOTICE BEFORE APPLYING A PESTICIDE FROM THE AIR

Under the Control of Pesticides Regulations 1986 (as amended) any person applying a pesticide from the air must do the following:

**56** AT LEAST 72 HOURS BEFORE STARTING THE TREATMENT YOU MUST DO THE FOLLOWING:

⬊ Consult the relevant conservation agency (Scottish Natural Heritage) if any part of a local nature reserve, marine nature reserve, a national nature reserve or a site of special scientific interest lies within 1500 metres of any part of the land to be treated;

⬊ Consult the appropriate area office of the Scottish Environment Protection Agency if the land to be treated is next to, or within 250 metres of, water;

⬊ Get permission from the Scottish Environment Protection Agency if the pesticide will be applied to control weeds in water or on the banks of watercourses or lakes.

**57** AT LEAST 48 HOURS BEFORE STARTING THE TREATMENT YOU MUST DO THE FOLLOWING:

⬊ Give notice to the appropriate reporting point of any local beekeepers' spray-warning scheme running in the district.

**58** AT LEAST 24 HOURS AND (AS FAR AS REASONABLY POSSIBLE) NO MORE THAN 48 HOURS BEFORE STARTING THE TREATMENT, GIVE NOTICE TO:

⬊ the local authority's Environmental Health Department;

⬊ the people occupying any property within 25 metres of the boundary of the land to be treated (or those people's agents); and

⬊ the person in charge of any hospital, school or other institution with boundaries lying within 150 metres of the flight path intended to be used for the treatment.

7

**59** AT LEAST 24 HOURS BEFORE STARTING THE TREATMENT YOU
MUST DO THE FOLLOWING:

⬃ Put sturdy and clear signs within 60 metres of the land to be treated to tell
people about the place, date and time of the treatment.

*You can find information on these and other legal conditions in the
Civil Aviation Authority (CAA) booklet 'Information on requirements
to be met by applicants and holders of the aerial application
certificate' (CAP 414).*

# ANNEX H

152 : PESTICIDES

THINGS TO CONSIDER WHEN PREPARING
AND MANAGING CONTRACTS FOR APPLYING
PESTICIDES IN AMENITY AREAS

## ANNEX H THINGS TO CONSIDER WHEN PREPARING AND MANAGING CONTRACTS FOR APPLYING PESTICIDES IN AMENITY AREAS

**60** If you are writing up or managing contracts for applying pesticides in amenity areas you should read the following guidance. It will help you to make sure that:

↘ all the work will be carried out in line with the relevant law; and

↘ the risks to people, wildlife and the environment will be assessed and adequately controlled.

### 61 PREPARING TENDERS

Anyone preparing a contract for pesticide to be applied should:

↘ take account of any relevant law; and

↘ consider the possible negative effects the pesticide may have on people, wildlife and the environment.

You should consider the following checklist when preparing land managing contracts. If you are not sure about anything, get expert advice.

### 62 POLICY ON USING PESTICIDES

↘ Have you considered alternative methods of control?

↘ Have you taken account of risks to people and the environment?

↘ Are you using the minimum amount of pesticides?

### 63 OBJECTIVE

↘ Do you have a clear understanding of the cause and effect of the problem to be treated?

↘ What does the contract aim to achieve?

### 64 LAWS

↘ Do you know and understand all relevant laws and codes of practice relating to supplying, storing and using pesticides?

### 65 EMPLOYEES

↘ Do you have enough trained and appropriately qualified staff and do they have the relevant expertise and knowledge?

### 66 PERFORMANCE STANDARD

↘ Do you want to set standards that must be met and put these in the contract?

## 67 AREAS FOR TREATING

↘ Have you defined the areas to be treated (including any relevant measurements, maps and plans)?

↘ Do your employees or the contractor know where sensitive and vulnerable areas (such as schools, hospitals, old people's homes, watercourses, sites of special scientific interest and nature reserves) are?

## 68 MONITORING

If you have a programme for monitoring the contract, can you make sure that:

↘ the conditions and standards of the contract are met; and

↘ appropriate records are kept.

## 69 REVIEW

↘ You should review all aspects of long-term contracts each year to make sure they act in line with any changes in policy, law, controls or any other factor that is likely to affect the contract.

## 70 MIXTURES

↘ Where you or an employee, contractor or supplier acting for you mixes pesticides with other substances, only enough mixture for the day's use should be made.

↘ However, unforeseen circumstances, such as bad weather conditions, may make it necessary to keep material for use in the next few days.

↘ If you have to keep material for use in the next few days, by law you or the contractor must make a new safety assessment on labelling and storing the mixture safely to make sure that, as far as is possible, no unacceptable risks are created.

↘ Do not store mixed products for long periods or in large amounts.

***Proper guidance on the law about selling and mixing pesticides is given in a leaflet available from PSD or on the PSD website (www.pesticides.gov.uk).***

## CONTRACT DETAILS

## 71 WORK TO BE CARRIED OUT

In the contract it would be a good idea to include a statement on the type and range of work to be carried out, with specific details of areas to be treated including:

↘ appropriate measurements;

↘ information on any unusual risks;

↘ any other proposed work (such as building work);

↘ any restrictions on working hours or machinery that may be used; and

↘ any specific instructions for working in or near sensitive or vulnerable areas.

## 72 CHOICE OF PESTICIDE

↘ In the contract you should specify the pesticide products to be used and their MAPP or HSE numbers (also written as active ingredients) and the rates of application.

↘ If you want the contractor to specify which pesticides they are going to use, you may want to ask them to give you a list of the pesticides (including MAPP or HSE numbers) they will use for each part of the contract, giving the application rates and number of treatments considered necessary.

## 73 REPORTING AND KEEPING RECORDS

↘ It is best practice for the contractor's representative on site to regularly report to your representative (perhaps once a week) to give you a detailed record of the work done and the plan for future work.

## 74 DOCUMENTS YOU MIGHT ASK CONTRACTORS TO PROVIDE

You may want the contractor to send you the following documents with their tender for the contract:

- A copy of their insurance certificates;

- The names and addresses of two referees they have carried out work of a similar type and value for;

- A copy of their storage certificate (unless less than 200 litres or 200 kilograms of pesticide are being stored);

- Copies of the appropriate NPTC certificates of competence for anyone who will be applying the pesticide or supervising the work;

- A copy of the contractor's safety policy, risk assessment and control procedures (as instructed under the Health and Safety at Work etc. Act and its associated regulations);

- Details of membership of any professional body or trade association;

- Details of the contractor's waste management policy;

- Details of the contractor's standard operating procedures (SOPs), directly related to the work as specified in the contract.

## 75 MONITORING CONTRACTS

It is good practice to monitor work carried out under contracts to make sure that all legal and safety conditions, and agreed standards, are met. A monitoring programme may cover the following:

## 76 PREPARING TENDERS

- Make sure that the contract schedules are an accurate record of the areas to be treated.

- Make sure the pesticides specified are adequate and suitable to achieve the aim of the treatment.

- Decide how often site inspections should take place.

- Prepare a checklist of the areas to be assessed during site inspections.

## 77 CARRYING OUT THE CONTRACT

When the contract is being carried out, you may want to visit all the sites to make sure of the following:

- The work is being carried out safely, legally and in line with relevant codes of practice;

- The people applying the pesticide are using suitable personal protective equipment and have the appropriate NPTC certificates of competence;

- The contractor's vehicles are suitably equipped to deal with any spillage or similar incident;

- The pesticides are being mixed and prepared in an appropriate location and in a safe and legal way;

- Only the people named in the documents provided with the tender are using pesticides;

- The pesticides being applied are as agreed in terms of the approved products, rates and method of application. (If any samples are tested, two samples should be taken, sealed immediately, and one should be left with the contractor.);

- All appropriate health and safety regulations are being followed;

- The pesticides are being stored on site in a safe and legal way;

- The appropriate records of the pesticides applied and the areas treated are being kept;

- All environmental risks are being managed appropriately;

- Written records are kept to show that leftover spray solution, tank washings and empty packaging are being disposed of safely, legally and in line with relevant codes of practice.

## 78 ASSESSING THE PERFORMANCE OF CONTRACTS

It is good practice to inspect all sites while the contract is being carried out and at appropriate intervals after it has ended to assess how effective the treatment is and, where necessary, ask the contractor to put things right.

# ANNEX I

**7** **THINGS TO CONSIDER WHEN USING PESTICIDES IN HIGH-SECURITY OR HIGH-RISK AMENITY AND INDUSTRIAL AREAS**

# ANNEX I THINGS TO CONSIDER WHEN USING PESTICIDES IN HIGH-SECURITY OR HIGH-RISK AMENITY AND INDUSTRIAL AREAS

79 You should take special care when applying pesticides in areas such as railways, gas and electricity plants, Ministry of Defence sites, oil refineries, public roads and motorways. This is because of the increased dangers at these sites and the need to take any extra safety precautions demanded at the site.

If you are supervising work on high-risk sites, you should fully understand:

↘ what work has to be done;

↘ how and when to contact the site's liaison officer;

↘ the local risks; and

↘ the safety precautions you must take as a result of the local risks (when working on public roads this will include meeting the Road Traffic Regulations).

80 You may also need to consider the following:

↘ Access to the site may be restricted to specific times, and certain types and sizes of vehicle may not be allowed;

↘ You may need a work permit or to be escorted on site;

↘ The controller of the site should supply you with all the relevant information and everyone involved should clearly understand the arrangements;

↘ You may want to agree appropriate penalties if you or the person who has to escort you does not arrive on schedule;

↘ Access routes to the site may be over land that is not controlled by the person who controls the site. You should make sure you have the permission you need to reach the site with the equipment you propose to use;

↘ For site security, visitors or your staff not directly involved in the work may only be allowed onto the site with the specific permission of the site controller (perhaps in writing).

As most of these sites are enclosed, it is best practice to see that you remove all rubbish and waste materials from site at the end of the work. You may want to have this done every day.

Special conditions apply to individual sites within any one contract. Make sure these are clear before you start work.

You should make sure any application equipment left on site is secure. If you leave any pesticides on site you must have the written permission of the site controller and they must be stored safely and securely.

The person supervising the work should contact local site controllers at least seven days before work is due to start to check whether:

↘ any special conditions apply to each site; and

↘ there will be other work in progress on the site while pesticides are being used.

81 You must not allow pesticides being applied to drift beyond the target area. If the weather conditions become unsuitable, stop work and tell the site controller what has happened.

# INDEX

NOTE: NUMBERS REFER TO
PARAGRAPHS, NOT PAGES.
NUMBERS WITH A LETTER
BEFORE THEM REFER TO
ANNEXES FOR EXAMPLE,
B11 IS PARAGRAPH 11 IN
ANNEX B).

8

# INDEX

Note: numbers refer to paragraphs, not pages. Numbers with a letter before them refer to annexes for example, B11 is paragraph 11 in annex B).

# E

8

# M

# N

# O

# P

# R

8

INDEX

# T

# U